Rooms of Grace

ROOMS OF GRACE

New and Selected Poems

Paul Petrie

NO
PJ

New Orleans Poetry Journal Press

ACKNOWLEDGEMENTS

The author wishes to thank the editors of the following books
and periodicals in which many of these poems first appeared:

*America, The American Scholar, Amicus, The Antioch Review,
Arizona Quarterly, The Atlantic, The Carleton Miscellany,
The Centennial Review, The Chicago Herald Tribune Magazine,
The Christian Century, The Christian Science Monitor,
The Colorado Quarterly, Commonweal,The Dark Horse, Epoch, Esquire,
Focus Midwest/70, The Gramercy Review, The Greyledge Review,
Hampden-Sydney Poetry Review,The Harvard Magazine,
Hellcoal Annual II, The Hollins Critic, The Hudson Review, Interim,
Kansas Quarterly, The Literary Review, The Little Magazine, The Lyric,
The Massachusetts Review, Michigan Quarterly Review,
The Minnesota Review, MSS, The Nation, Negative Capability,
New Campus Writing No. 2, New England Review,
New Orleans Poetry Journal, The New Republic,
The New York Herald Tribune, The New York Times,
The North American Review, The Northeast Journal,
Northwest Review, The Ontario Review, The Paris Review, Poetry,
Poetry Review, Poetry Ireland, Prairie Schooner, Raritan,
The Rhode Islander, Roanoke Review, San José Studies,
The Saturday Review of Literature, The Sewanee Review,
Shenandoah, South Carolina Review, Southern Humanities Review,
The Southern Review, Southwest Review, Stand, The Texas Review,
The Treasury of American Poetry, The Transatlantic Review and Yankee.*

"Bridge Park," "The Enigma Variations," "From Under the Hill of Night,"
"Identity," "The Message," and "The Old Pro's Lament" first appeared in
The New Yorker.

Previously published poetry collections from which a great number
of these poems were selected are:

Confessions of a Non-Conformist, Hillside Press, Mt Vernon, Iowa, 1963.
The Race With Time and the Devil, A selection of the Book Club for Poetry, Golden
Quill Press, Francestown, NH, 1965.
From Under the Hill of Night, Vanderbilt University Press, Nashville,
Tennessee, 1969.
The Academy of Goodbye, The University Press of New England, Hanover,
NH, 1974.
Light From the Furnace Rising, Copper Beech Press, Brown University, 1978.
Time Songs, The Biscuit City Press, Kingston, RI, 1979.
Not Seeing Is Believing, Juniper Press, La Cross, WI, 1983.
Strange Gravity, The Tidal Press, Cranberry Isles, ME, 1984.
The Runners, Slow Loris Press, PA, 1988. (Selected for The Capricorn Award)

I would also like to thank my family, Kimberly Whittington, my designer, and especially my editor, Maxine Cassin, for their invaluable help.

The cover illustration is Johannes Vermeer's *Woman Holding a Balance*, Widener Collection, Image © Board of Trustees, National Gallery of Art, Washington, DC.

Published by New Orleans Poetry Journal Press, 2131 General Pershing St., New Orleans, LA 70115.

ISBN# 0-938498-10-X

Library of Congress Catalog Number 2005922548.

CONTENTS

On Looking at a Vermeer

II. Portraits, Histories and Mythologies

III. Songs and Other Measures

IV. The World of Ideas

PREFACE

A note is perhaps necessary to explain the organization of
the poems in this collection. Usually volumes of this sort
are arranged chronologically, according to the date of
composition or publication. Instead I have chosen to group
these pieces by subject matter or genre.

There are four major sections in the book. The first and
longest is more or less autobiographical and traces the
development of a life from childhood to old age. The poems
were not written with this in mind so there are various
anomalies in terms of pronouns, facts, times and places, and
there are certainly notable omissions, but the hope here is to
produce that narrative interest which even a life as relatively
uneventful as mine may afford.

In the second section the poems are more objective and
dramatic. The characters and situations are taken from my
own observations and imaginings, as well as from history and
mythology.

The title of the third part, *Songs and Other Measures*, pretty
well describes its contents. Nearly all the poems employ rhyme
and meter, some very freely, and, though not technically songs,
aim at the musical effects that songs can achieve.

The pieces in the final section are mostly concept-centered,
with the usual exceptions and discrepancies. They are grouped
according to large subject areas such as The Mind, Art,
Symbols and Allegories, Nature, etc.

In all the sections the placing of the individual poems has
been long and carefully considered, and the aim is that, so
arranged, each poem will make its maximum emotional and
imaginative effect. Whether this is so or not, these are some of
the best fruits of a long lifetime of poetic labor, and I hope that
reading them will give you that sense of heightened life and joy
which is the natural function and blessing of art.

This book is dedicated to all those writers, artists, and composers, both living and dead, who have added so much happiness to my life. My debt and my gratitude are immeasurable. Whenever I get discouraged by world events, or dismayed by my own follies or the follies of my kind, I have only to think of them and hope comes flooding back.

ON LOOKING AT A VERMEER

It mirrors me—as if it did not hold
that woman weighing pearls and weighed with child,
and I, this wintry beard, were domiciled
in that dusk-pregnant, summer's room of gold.

But images are mad. Reflections break
into this bronze retreat; and my whole room
pursues me here—here in this amber gloom
two rooms contend and wrestle for my sake.

There is a cave, whose winding, backward coils
lead, if all maps are fables, to this place.
That labyrinth deciphered, this dark face
shall roll in those golden scales, a pearl in pearls.

I.

FRAGMENTS FROM A LIFE

1

A trifle turned my head, and there it was:
frivolous with light, crisscrossed with streams
that raced their running banks, confused with blooms
stung by hired bees to colored towns,
a sudden land of wings that flew like birds.
(But farther in the forest, busy night
hangs her purple mischief on the trees,
and Long John Silver stumps the pirate glades
scything black-eyed Susans with his leg.)
There, within a bird-shot of their hearts,
a boy and girl once chased the stiff-legged clouds,
tamed the rolling hills, ran down the wind,
and dared the sun to do them into gold.

I would not turn young virgins into flame;
but time will hear its ribald pranks retold.
Once in a berry bush where bears were not,
a boy and girl were picking royal blue
and even to their ears were kings and queens,
when in flew a backward thief who could not tell
a flower from a boy, and gave a sting
where pain cannot be covered by a blush.

All sympathy and tears, she would have spent
her very bluest plunder for his ease,
but hurt with a more-than-mortal wound he ran
to quench his scarlet image in the lake.

Night drew off the valley's face of dreams.

He never circled back. Some said Le Fey
took him in her swan boat like the king,
and some that Long John pressed him off to sea,
but I, who knew the boy and still can find
when trifles turn my head that country,
imagine that no magic filched his heart,
although I call his name and hear the hills.

CHILD'S DREAM SONG

Out of the upstairs window
I step upon the air
and walk across the tops of trees
without a care.

Birds in their leafy cages
suspend their whistlings
to see this strange bird walking by
without its wings.

And people and cars far under
stop in their mazy ways,
craning their necks straight upwards
and stare, amazed.

Over the gull-winged towers,
over bunched hills I go,
strolling across the backs of clouds
like drifts of snow.

Then passing the last horizon,
I turn and walk back home,
step in through my bedroom window
back to my own room.

"Are you there, spider?" we said, hurling flies still buzzing
into that trembling web.
                    And sure enough—
first at the spiral hole, then with sudden pounce
which always surprised, invisible ballet steps,
out he would come, examine the proffered gift,
inject the poison neatly behind the neck
and parcel up the body.
                    For days we fed
fly after fly into those gossamer strands,
hands poised upon walls, the pores of walks,
the hot, enameled, shining tops of rails,
till the flies were all used up.
                        And the web grew dark
with the shrouded bodies of flies (some slowly withering
in the speckled eye of the sun, their blood unsucked)
and the spider slower to come.
                        And then, one day,
did not.
                    "Are you there, spider?" we said, hurling
pebbles, beetles, ants, small bits of stick
into that bulging net, hungry to see
once more that ballet leap, those closing jaws,
the neatly shrouded corpse—until the web
sagged with the weight
                    and broke—
                                and with our hands
we swept it away.

                    And still no spider came.

THE DEFENDER OF ANIMALS

Snakes were my closest friends.

Under the willows' plumes—liquescent, green—
I'd watch them tend their young, herding them down
at the slightest warning into those slant black holes
between the willows' roots;
or lie in the warm June fields and see them bathe
in open places, or on the backs of rocks,
their heads moving vaguely in a sun-blind daze.

Or take them home in jars
and teach them to crawl
over the length of my arm with a dry tickling,
or coil round my neck like pearls—
forbidden, cool.

I was a king and my people were the snakes.
With swaying heads upraised they'd come to me
to be stroked gently between their yellow eyes,
or flicker their tongues
into my cupped-up palms.

And when gangs of boys
caught them with sticks
and tied them to the streetcar tracks
to be chopped to bits,
I'd set them free or, failing,
gather the severed parts and with secret rites
bury them, one by one, in hidden graves,
each part
to come alive.

But in good time,
all kings and their kingdoms end.

Now where the fields once were there is a school,
and over the bulldozed hills, packed gravel-hard,
children run, playing—
skinning their knees and laughing, rolling hoops and balls.
The willows have gone—with all their secret graves—
and the snakes gone down
under the earth so deeply that even I
am afraid to put my hand in those mouthless holes.

GLANCES

To see—
        and not to see—

Soft, women's voices—
The bedroom door ajar—
Silks slithering down—
And I in the livingroom too young to count.

My eyes fixed on the clock's
gold-moving hands,
admonishing—

But glances—sudden glimpses—
                           Swaying breasts—
White buttocks shining out like wintry moons—
Soft tapered arms—
                And then my cousin's body
fully seen—
            pink-mounded belly,
brown nest of frizzly hair,
                plump, gleaming thighs—

The clock's gold-moving hands
admonishing—

            And again in the same year
that moon-like pallor—
under the stiff, rouged mask
of the face—
           pale, waxen arms—
One glance into the coffin passing by.

Grey rain, black tossing trees, dark flowing clouds—

The wooden chest lowered in the dripping hole—

Inside, my cousin's body—
                dazzling, white—
hidden from all eyes.

ADVENTURE

The streetcar jerks and sways on its metal rails.
The hand-straps bang the roof.

Against the grimy window he leans one cheek
and peers into the night.
His stop is soon.
Shapeless the dark floods by,
pierced by the yellow eyes of hidden
houses,
            and streetlights on the corners, iron-masked,
and stiff as priests.

Around the bend they sway. His stop is next.
He stands on the wicker seat and pulls the cord—
but no sound comes. And again
he tugs at the yellow cord, but still
no sound—
            "Conductor," he wants to cry— "Conductor, stop!"
but his tongue sticks in his mouth, no words escape—
and on through the swaying dark the streetcar rushes
on its iron rails.
Tears start to his eyes. He yanks at the cord
with all his strength—hangs on like a drowning man.
A distant, wheezy buzz—
The wheels screetch on the rails—grind stop—The doors fold back—
and out he stumbles
into the moth-winged night.

One mile back,
among those dark-clumped houses
is his house. With beating heart,
he begins the long journey through alien lands—
past an Esso station, bathed in an unreal light—
past a small grocery, in its window a giant clock
with greenly glowing hands—
under the whispering branches
of elms—

The air is warm, thick, full of lilac scent.
The moon floats on the roofs. White stars lean down.
In the distance, familiar lights.
With every step he grows more sure,
more brave,
and halfway home,
hands tucked in his pockets, he begins
whistling.
And when the streetcar going the other way
glides past,
            he watches those moving lights
till they disappear, around the far-off bend.

The smell of castor oil—
                    Small figure hunched
over the oil-cloth's white and yellow squares
in the breakfast nook,
                    moving the salt and pepper
back and forth—
                    "Then stay there till you do!"—
the glittering spoon, propped on a cereal bowl,
brimful of that cat's evil yellow oil—

Can I believe, small boy, that you stayed till noon,
from breakfast time till the factory whistle blew,
while blackbirds, robins, jays fluttered in the basswood,
and from the vacant lot, five houses down,
came the shouts of boys, quarreling the game of baseball?

Heroic shade,
I stare at your hunched, round-shouldered misery,
(one spoonful from delight)
and smile—

But swelling in my throat and chest still feel
oppression's bitter ache,

taste in my mouth the cold, sweet taste
of pride.

Once, in the kingdom of summer,
lying beneath three trees
I watched the curled, slow-moving clouds
drift at their ease.

And watched the cloud-fringed branches
nod in the summer's air,
turning the leaves to shields of light
white-flashing there.

Wherever those clouds were going,
they were going at their own pace,
careless of days—of destinations
in some other place.

Cicadas sang in the branches.
Tree toads opened their throats.
Birds from their three green towers dropped
enchanted notes.

Behind me, an endless summer.
Ahead, long summer days—
lengthening into twilight's deep,
blue mysteries.

Once, in the kingdom of summer,
lying in the summer's grass
I watched the curled, slow-moving clouds—
that passing, never passed.

"Deboissart's Real Estate," and underneath
in red neon "STAMPS."
                          The one with the flowing sleeves
and spectacles, leaning on the long glass counter—
"Which book today?" I point to an enormous tome
which she hoists down, turning the pages slowly
with jeweled, ritual hand.
                          The Archduke winks
through his gold pince-nez—Astrid, Queen of Belgium
shines from black borders—The snakes, giraffes, rhinos
of Liberia—Tana Tuva's diamond peaks—
                                    (Coins
in my pocket slither and sweat.)
                          "Now please, The United
States."
           Ben Franklin's ultramarine, rose Jackson,
the voyages of Columbus (sixteen stamps),
Mount Zion, Yellowstone, The Grand Canyon—
The book closes—I abandon hope, and choose.

Then the long walk back through miles of turning streets,
guarding my shining packet—
                          Each stamp removed
with silver tongs, gummed hinges folded, licked—
then into their destined spaces, each bright picture
pressed—

                    where still they wink and glow—exotic lands—
fabulous countries where no man's ever been.

14

THE GARDENER

And there were the roses, drenching the summer's air
with a thousand shining scents—
                              And there was the roses'
keeper, stoop-backed, wrinkle-faced, with a gold-toothed smile,
pruning the red-barbed stems, picking off the blossoms
that were overripe, and searching the tight-sheathed buds
for aphids, beetles, grubs—
                              I walked beside,
small shadow on the dew-soaked lawn, while on
he talked—of Buddha, Gandhi, Tolstoy, Jesus
Christ—all the morning prophets of the world—
not understanding much, but understanding
that this was the garden and this the garden's keeper
whose very hands were wise, and running from rose to rose
drinking in the fragrant ichors of the sun.

If I say he had a wife who was a scold,
that his children grew up neither rich nor happy,
that he played favorites, worked all his life at McClery's
fixing stoves, and died at last unknown
I speak as a sworn witness, now that those crimson
ears are underground, to what prodigious magic,
drifting through summer mornings, those roses heard.

Weaving through the long shadows—
in and out they go
in unreflective arcs
of bodily delight,
or stand—pumping—still
as the dark ghosts of trees.

It is June. The sun is low.
Blue houses cross the street,
and back and forth they glide,
now drowned in shadow,
now smeared by the late sun
a shy and unruly gold.

They will dismount soon, I know,
and clustered in dark bushes
under the bending scents
of night, lilac and strange,
play their exotic games.

But in my mind still go
in soft, elliptic circles
through light and back, through shadow,
archaic, rich, beyond
all memory and pain.

And shall continue so
always, gliding the streets
of a long-dead summer,
though the doors lean out and call,
and the gaps of houses close.

THE TRIP TO THE ISLAND

The streets rush down to the river.
The horns of morning blow
three, white-plumed blasts—
and up the gangplank rumbles
on the Bob-Lo boat.

Like snakes the hawsers coil
through the oil-filmed waters.
Slowly the shore drifts off.
Towers of the city shrink
into the sky—

Sun on the top deck. Breezes
that blow the hair of girls
halfway to Canada.
White napkin-covered baskets
bulging with meats and cakes.
The sounds of children running
down the passageways—
of the Bob-Lo boat.

Below deck, limes and cherries
spin their lucky fruit.
The floor throbs with the engines.
There's the smell of steam and brass,
and up and down in their wells
the pistons churn green waters
white.

All morning stacks of factories
loom and fade,
white hills of sand and lime,
and then the long, low forearms
of marshy land—
the wide blue burst of the waves—
from the Bob-Lo boat.

Night cruises meant for lovers.
Torches of foundries leaping
into the dark,
casting their soft-webbed shadows.
The shy meeting of lips.
The Columbiad of hands—

Small islands gliding past
like turtles' backs.
The low-strung lights of freighters
moving between the cold,
sharp-featured stars
and the sheeted light of the moon—
from the Bob-Lo boat.

The island's still and dark—
only a few bulbs burning
among the trees.
Horses of the merry-go-round
hang on air. All the booths
are shut. It is late. It is late,
as we slip ashore
and cluster on the dock.

Three long deep blasts on the whistle.
Again the white plumes tower.
Tiered lights drift off and shrink
into the long night sky,
and we stand at the lake's edge watching
those jeweled lights fade, and waving
to the Bob-Lo boat.

THE THROW

Last of the ninth—two out, three on,
the ball
snaking in from the mound, the sharp
crack of the bat, the white
sphere, bounding in one clean
arc, leaping like a homing pigeon
into my mit,
one arm thrown back,
the throw—
(the batter dropping his bat, his legs moving
slow-motion—all the time—all the time
in the world)—
straight, bullet-hard and true
toward the outstretched glove—
but rising, rising—
as if on wings, a freed bird, into air—

Like clockwork men,
runners circling the bases,
and the ball still rising—
over the first-baseman's head—
over the dugout with its upturned
eyes—and the runners circling the bases,
crossing the plate—one run, two runs,
three—and the game
is through, the West Side playoffs
lost, and the ball still rising—

All the way home in the car,
head bent, eyes glazed with shame—
and in my dreams that night
the ball still rising—

never to land
except in some far-off field
light years away
upon the grave of honor, glory,
baseball—

and from the earth a sprig of flowers
rising—sweet laurel crown.

In the dark room with grief
made musical, and pain
swelling the moist body
of night, till the night seemed,
for all its aching lamps
and cold archways, rich,
and the full moon—rising—
proof of the heart's size,
how could he then foresee
himself—grown-up—a man,
turning on a damp bed
like a child, tears burrowing
in, both head and throat
turned stone, and pressing down
upon each breath he breathed,
like shame, or a bad memory,
the intolerable body of loss.

BRIDGE PARK

This is the place where summer comes to sleep:
the men bare-necked, the women dressed for bed—
their hair in snarls, their children half in tears—
to stand, or sit, or lie at river's edge
and catch the breezes, fanned by burning steel.
The bridge is there—opening other lands,
its lights upon the waters, spilling moons,
but few regard the bridge, or watch its lines.
Most strain their eyes on spider strings of lights
that look like shore, but move, unlike the shore,
upstream, or down, and on, and out of sight,
where still the horns give substance to the past.

I think of Avalon and Arthur's barge,
of how the horns bring loneliness to bear,
of how the lights might fit on Christmas trees,
though white and far from shore, of going somewhere—
and wipe my sweating head. They watch the ships:
their lights, names, motion, and feel the heat
leave their clammy skins and go inside.

The sea was calm.
He swam
until the green was stone
he could not dint,
and his arms stretched far away
on another body;
then ceased and hung
on the steep edge of the sea.

The sky was a black lid
holding a distant voice
suspended in the sea.
And when he sank, the stars
spiraled past his head
in silver wells;
and the fish
had an odd look in their serious eyes.

She was bent
over the deranged bed,
her eyes great growing pools
of concern.

Not since a child
had he cried aloud in his sleep.

2

So many waving hands before the last,
when from the deck, leaning, you watch the dark
pull down those desperate, white, surrendering flags,
and turn to claim the land of never-leaving.
Practice must have some efficient end.
We grow so skillful in the arduous rites.
Each sun must have its words, each falling star;
each ticking of the great clock swings goodbye.

The girl whose mother gave me cookies died
when I was four; and even then, without
a catechism of defeats, I knew
the face the heart must make, the shape of tears.
Subtleties have mastered me since then.
I've learned to know when hands must signal arcs
of epic loss, or when despair will do,
but nothing grows more perfect but the pain.

Now I leave my home—a small hand-wave,
and yet the rhetoric of parting builds
with such enormous lendings from the past,
I can't escape without a cheating tear.

Why must we learn so well?—Because the end
is such a grave goodbye it must be done
with more than just a single perfect act
(the dead go fast, and some lack even hands),
or is there no country that never ends?

FUNERAL SUITE

In memory of my sister-in-law,
Nancy Petrie, 1919-1953

1. The Journey

The call came in the dead of night.
A pink ghost in a fumbling gown.
Bare feet pitting the stairs—circling down,
down. The receiver clattered. The light

snapped on. It spread like lies, like news,
after the first gasp and sputter.
No one believed it—a window shutter
banging in the wind. We couldn't refuse

our roles, but the quiet, backstage fact...
Had come too shy by morning to
be false, was still too real to be true.
We serviced the car, packed.

The day was sunny. Talking, joking,
we left, but soon took on the face
we feared was fit. North. Our fingers traced
their tremble on our knees. Our throats

began to fight their hollows. The bread
and salmon tasted mealy.
The air smelled dark. Fidgeting, we began to feel
the odd distance of the dead.

2. The Funeral Parlor

The funeral director probed our names,
and finding we were privileged to suffer
led us to the brilliant cradle smothered
in flowers and satin. "What a shame!"

They passed on by us. "She died so young."
Mother crept to the casket side
on tip-toe. We followed, hoping to hide
our eyes within her tears. A numb

precaution. No one we had known.
Some cleaning woman perhaps—puffed hands,
false hair—a fortune-teller, a vendor—not Nan.
We turned our backs to show we could not own

relation, and browsed among the flowers—
not what we paid for the price.
The ones sent by her Company ... Twice
the cards were scored—the names to honor,

the names that forgot. The parlor emptied.
Fumes of supper drifted through the doors,
from the rooms upstairs.
We loitered, waiting for that face to cede

its falsehood. No muscle stirred. The head
slowly began to crush the living bone.
Terrified, we turned and left her—alone,
a stranger to the live and to the dead.

3.   The Funeral

They lined us up by weight of tears.
The bell tolled us in to seats
near death. She was the centerpiece
in a rich display; of all the blooms there

not the most wilted. We sat. The choir
began its questions on the lines
of a dog-eared text. The pine
boards cut our bones. The candles wept fire.

I watched my brother, taking my cue
from his rainproof face. The women did
the crying. The preacher bid
for our souls, hoping the fever and stew

would make us forget our dead Christians.
We forgot them, and received the spurious heaven
gratefully. A few words of historical leaven,
incorrect in Finnish and English—unction

for the dead. She took it with a careless grace,
expecting dissatisfaction; but we,
disenchanted, frightened, fled to retrieve
the slandered past, while a prayer paced

at our heels like a Fury. A singer sang
in scalding tones a cold song.
The organ howled in Finnish and English. Long
lines filed by the captive face—rank

on rank. And we were alone by the oak bed.
Words, prayers, tears, songs forgotten,
we stood, looking down at the garden
of our exile, from the land of the dead.

4. The Burial

The cars groaned up the last hill,
coughing their ghosts on the white air,
and turned at the broken gate, bearing
the black box to its earthen till.

We bundled from the warm shell to the cold
and huddled in fists by the grave.
The bearers brought out the coffin and laid
it dangerously on the mouth of the dark hole.

The preacher spoke of the fate of the good.
The blast wrenched his words to spinning
leaves. All you could hear was the wind
rasping its talons through the tangled wool of the woods.

We shivered, crouching deeper into collars.
No eye was free from a clot of tears
cracked from a frozen will. The clear
air made our lungs ache. A prayer streamed by like anger.

"Ashes to ashes..." The wind reclaimed the dust.
The preacher grasped my brother's hand
and shook it through the glove—the others'. The band
broke up. We ran for the cars. The rest

through the ice window—Nan being put to bed;
the slow settling—down—down—
The engine coughed and sputtered. The ground
shivered at the touch of the dead.

5. Afterwards

Back in the ragged living room,
worn by the child years of one
whom we had put to earth, loss began
to take its human shape. The monstrous gloom

was chased under the sofa by the dog.
Apple-jack sprang from the hearty kegs.
Set in a half circle, we stretched our legs
to the fire; and from the curling logs

a child leaped up before us: climbing
the next-door oak to steal the robin
blind, and leaving a penny for ransom,
so blue they were, so blue. Chiming

the cows' bells, and tying their tails
to trees, but brushing the flies from their backs,
and scolding Josiah for nibbling their hocks
when he fetched them. Walking the rails

of the orchard and teasing the masterless ram,
a child leaped up before us. My brother's
eyes burned in the dark, and he talked of a later
girl. We listened, approving, damned

by a mindless lust, forgetting how dangerously
the past dwindled. The wedding came
and went—leaves fell and fell—flames
crumbled in their ashes—the hours streaked by—

Time gathered its tongues and struck—and the live past fled—
And there in the dark, a child leaped up before us,
stretching to our power through a grappling forest
a cold bird—to lift it from the dead.

Our mittened hands upon the snow-capped stone,
we stood and watched what once was river zag
a black and crazy trickle through the ice.
The bridge was not enough to heal the gap
that severs brothers' hands. Our minds were one.
Her patience was a hopeless miracle.
Boxed in a narrowness she always feared,
and housed in solid cold she was too thin
to stand, she took it kindly, like herself,
who all that day had not been like herself.
The music might have pleased her; even more
these named, familiar trees, this cobbled stream
that from her youth had memorized her face.

Defined and dared, she seemed to stand again
between us, almost touching, leaning down,
her chin cupped in her hands, her eyes upon
the nighthawks tracking the falling light, and glad,
its show of protest through, the purple sun
would drop into the stream and make it warm.

My brother sent her home: "It's almost dark,"
and turning, brushed his arm against my side.
The snow squealed under foot as if in pain.
The trees looked black, the bridge half-shadowy;
but we were not deceived: the bridge was stone.

To leave a stone that will not last the night;
To keep a trust unkept by the faithless dead;
To cleanse my tears, or lack of them, I write
these words which will not pierce your soundless bed.
The book they should have swelled, you placed half-read
upon the shelf and snapped the reading light.

I used to mock you, Nan, for thumbing back
to steal the end before you earned its wages.
The sad you never read. Fastidious girl,
what ending made you shy this sunny book
and leave your loved ones wandering empty pages—
live characters without their living world?

YOUNG LOVER'S SONG

For Sylvia

Uncurtain the sun! Rouse up the moon!
This inward light's too fierce to bear—
faces of houses, faces of people
flashing their white fires on the air.

Streets end—the ends are all beginnings.
Buildings rise up on cloudy wings.
I stand on the corner and lift one finger—
blessings fall upon all things.

Why are my feet so full of dancing?
Why has my tongue gone mad with joy?
It takes two hands to hold this body
from floating upwards, through the sky.

Sweet sorceress, what spell is this?
What secret, all-entrancing charm
that turns the whole world magic, magic
wrapped in the white wands of your arms?

Renoir or Cezanne; it came to that.
But slumped across the tragic wicker chair
that gnawed her trousseau slip; and thunder-backed,
hanging ties like martyrs on the wall;
they could not even find their quarrel out,
let alone be plausible in tears.
They might have dodged by several ready feints;
but still themselves, and young, and close to fact,
they could not come too close to what they felt,
or hide it in a name it wasn't called.
And so they ached, till she gave up her pride
in naming things, and wept their difference whole.

They learned as much as lovers ever learn
this side of love; but still, the central flaw
of space was touched.
                              Those Frenchmen and their fruit!
Why will they put their worlds in separate bowls,
where the young can pick the apples up and bite?

In separate cages, oh my Love,
we keep our striped identities,
and celebrate across cool bars
our sensual amenities.

We know the tricks of claws, and know
how cages brighten lovers' charms,
but in our dreams how all worlds lie
tiger to tiger in our arms.

The good fist opens—lawns,
music, trips and friends
talking of nothing, blue skies
stippled with feathery signs
white-drifting onwards—

           And books,
and dreams, and poems—

           And again
I am poured like a child's soldiers
from the indigo box, and stand
luxurious with days
in rich stances—

         And once more
begin the breath-taking climb
to goodness, joy, and fame.

AUTUMN EVENING

Personally, for us, the sun has roofed
these houses with his golden agonies.
The ivy talks its thousand cheeping tongues.
To us the basswood throws the lucky leaves.

Catastrophe is just around the corner.
Clouds have passed through storm and back again.
One hand that trembles on the light—Eclipse!
One turn across the room—the world ends.

My wife is beating egg-yolks in a bowl.
I set the knives and forks beside the plates.
Our bodies touch, and turning, touch and kiss—
too long, too hard, the universe will break.

My work may be for birds' nests, hers a way
of manning ground already championed.
The steaks cry out: "Tonight we eat in black!"
The act cannot be measured by its end.

We sit and say the grace, not so convinced
of numbered hairs, but thankful for the praise.
The meat is somewhat better for the black.
The window ushers in a proud blaze.

SARDINE BOATS

(Mallorca)

Just as a shoe falls on the bedroom floor
their bass pug-pug arrests us. Staring out
we see them, tiny stars to mark the ship,
and great round glaring eyes for the working boats
that string behind, a fleet of lemon moons.
We go to bed, half-awed and half-ashamed
(and deeply aware of weariness and the night)
that boats could be such better men than we.
We sleep. All night, above the swimming dark,
they sieve the inky depths for what they hold.

They say the fish, when hauled up to the moon,
shine out with such a brightness eyes can see
by silver scales, by wriggling life alone.
We dream; but bring up such a fishy brood
we'll flaunt them later over jam and toast
only to cleanse our hands of such a catch.
But back with the dawn they come, with deeper songs,
chorused with gulls that flap about their wake
like tattered sails, and steam across our vision
into the waking harbor with the sun.
And we arise, into an accomplished world.

I met you at our wedding, shook your hand
and bowed to the laughing smile that was your wife.
You were a jokester, buoyant, full of life.
You decked our bumper, siphoned out our tank.
Now, on a swaying trolley in a foreign land,
I hear that you have played your final prank.

At first the cancer struck a private vein.
At night, in bed, what stifled speech, in tears,
one world of love split to neuter spheres,
what cries of unbelief, what vows till death!
The knife cut in and took away all pain.
And then—the moths—crowding the rooms of breath.

The day the doctors told you you would die
you took the long way home, through Eldon Park,
and watched the elm trees sift the growing dark,
streetlights in the pond swell out and spill,
and bought three orange custards and a pie.
The stones you walked on echoed, and were still.

Now you are safe from echoes, darkness' friend.
The hand I grappled has unclasped the world
and lies upon the lap of time, uncurled.
A graver cancer eats away all trace
of that strong heart, and all your humours end
in just two furrows upon a woman's face.

The trolley bucks and shudders—you are gone—
and I get off to face the city's night.
Shadows crowd around each naked light,
and echoes of my footsteps fill the street.
Cousin, goodbye—I know you—we are kin.
The heart admits another small defeat.

Standing on the white threshold,
rungs of the metal pail
still printing his hands, his eyes
huge saucers brimming behind
the guarded lids,
he lingered—lights of her thighs
still warm in his glance, the lean,
lucid, sea-scooped brow,
and down the violet passage
the arm of the bearded man
splashing reds, yellows, umbers
on the taut, breathless spaces—
till the steps returned, the coin
closed on his fist, and he cycled
down the rising mountain of dreams.

HOME VOYAGE

The hawsers drop like anchors in the sea,
but cannot hold the shore. It drifts away.
We wave our hands—to taxis, windmills, grey
cathedral spires. Like aging memory
the island shrinks into the dying day.
Its tallest mountains barely top our foam.
The world turns and drowns our second home.

Our hill will miss us; suns go poor to bed
without the tribute of our eyes; this sea
vary its twelve-tone music fruitlessly;
and Torre Ros rear up its castled head
without conferring wealth and royalty.
Such happiness strikes only once, like grace.
This place will bear a scar and we a place.

Now, journeying back where houses know us best—
to our own land, home town where every street
echoes the childish patterns of our feet,
and in one room, like ingots in a chest
of pirate gold, all childhood memories meet—
we come as visitors, afraid the cracks
will fell the walls before we turn our backs.

Two nights ago we saw this ship, ablaze,
a house of many rooms, all rich with light,
and saw it dwindle, fade, and drop from sight,
sliding down the rim of dark, amazed
that houses now could move and ride the night.
Two homes have gone, heaved anchor up and sailed.
We lose ourselves piecemeal across the world.

The waves refuse the moonlight all repose,
tilt up the deck and slant the starboard rails.
Emitting plangent cries, our whistle hails
a line of distant lights that comes and goes.
The stars move in the sky; the white moon sails;
and this round world flees backward into foam—
where gulls build on the waves a constant home.

RITES IN OCTOBER

(Peru, Nebraska)

I dance before my boy—long spindle bones
aclick like castinets, stilt legs that bend
in slinky stances, Oh Professor P.　!—
a Spanish dance who cannot dance a step.
And double up to see my son's delight,
his face one spreading crimson moon of joy,
true flattery for folly, his first laugh.

Against the shade the headlong leaves plunge down,
like capsized hands, or birds that lose the air,
or resurrected, spin and twist in the wind.

I fling him up into the indoor sky—
his eyes grow little worlds—he plunges home
shrieking to happiness, and hugs my sides.
Like birds that tumble on the October air
we roll upon the floor, unravelling joy
like balls of colored twine. Against my face
his face is soft and warm.
　　　　　　　　　Outside, the wind
plucks the trees of their most feathered pride.

A fountain in the afternoon,
his huge bulk molten,
he held me with his bony eye
and, mopping the cliff of his face
with his red bandana,
his belly rumbling beer—
"I should like to die."
I put him in the movies,
and smiled,
though he gave no cue.
But all the way home,
like a boy on his long laces,
I tripped on our common words.
At the doorway he nodded,
and I watched him climb
up the dank stairs—
back laboring,
his damp shirt fading
into the oblong of space.
Two months later,
on the cracked bathroom floor,
an enormous puddle of red
launching
a brief letter.

And I remember,
lunging at the car door
with incredible meaning
the tall, bony girl
whom by the hem of her skirt
I seized,
shuddering to the curb
in blind confusions of hate,
and silently scolding, scolding, wondering
what was there on the street,
what was there on the stone street
for a girl, and a lover?

And now, again, last night—
his jaw clipped and working—
the old monotonous words
of misery and self-hate
falling,
falling,
upon deaf ears.

Logic brandished like a stick
in forced tones
over a sweating stomach—
but reeling by, the dark miles,
the invincible canyons.

O fountained Tree,
rooted in the sun,
with your green nerves
and lyric branches,
or conjugations of form,
what have you done to my friends
that they should wish to dangle
from black boughs,
unnatural fruit?

Instruct me, teach me,
that love may attend them
to the head of the stairs;
or must I also
see the oak scarecrow
limping up the hill of the sky,
shedding on the wind
the nest of his brains?

The afternoon slants in and gilds the spoon
my father waves to lead the birthday song,
my brother pounds the table like a gong,
we raise our glasses: "To that time-saving one ..."
and you are pleased. You purse your lips, to say
that pleasure must be measured to be long,
not frittered out in smiles. The table's gay
with blooms and colored napkins. The cake is bright,
each candle burning one decade of light.
Too many years have gone to make this day.

I see it all, young Scrooge brought back by love,
and join the burning festival of praise,
but fear those dwindling lights, unthrift of days.
One year while we are bawling joy you'll move
softly to a house whose stones are gilt
with constancies no wind or fire can raze;
and then our house will fall: the table tilt,
the dishes smash, the doors swing out and hurl
us derelicts to the streets that rove the world.
You are the rock on which our house is built.

Strange birthday song—for death; you will not die.
You used to sit beside me on the bench
and box my ears to music. And I would clench
my fists, pounding the stubborn keys, and cry.
That music, set to words, is what I bring.
And there are subtler ways. Time could not quench
the thirst you raised in us for mastering
its tricks and sleights. What's lost is what must last
by grip of the heart alone. There is no past.
Permanence is a never-ending thing.

My gifts from you, upon your birthday—queer!
I come at Christmas time (biennially)
to find new presents bending down the tree,
and childhood like an unstuffed teddy-bear.
I am too old. Saint Nicholas is not true.
Fame I brandish: our name eternally,
blazed on the pages schoolboys suffer through.
You nod and smile: fame is a little room

within the living heart. My wings? The plume
I put in time's grey cap? Old gifts from you.

Guilt has many birthdays; you, but one.
I give up all pretense to justify
my life (The world was never just. The sky
turns black and blue.) and own myself, your son.
There was a child, one spring, who saw a star
drop down as if bright heaven were a lie,
and wept because the shining world was marred.
His mother took a coin and tossed it—up—
and up— . You smile. Happy birthday! The cup
has come around. I give you—what you are.

CONFESSIONS OF A NON-CONFORMIST

(West Kingston, R.I.)

At fourteen
I decided to be
unorthodox,
a man
who sings for his bread,
and likes bread,
who cheats himself on his taxes,
and who would have been
first to the moon,
but on arriving
has forgotten his flag.

My mother shrieked,
and dropped her iron
on the foot of the stove.
My father reached
for his razor-strap and his wallet.
The cat yawned.

I eat carrots
in public places.
I carry spiders
out-of-doors
on the Sunday paper.
I am unfriendly with my banker.
But still wonder.
God-fearing? Free? White? Thirty-one?
Certainly afraid. I fall down cliffs in my dreams.
I support a dentist
single-handed,
and have not yet mastered
the art of breathing
underground.

The basswood seeds
litter the walks,
and Philip, my son, the king
lifts one knee in vain
to avoid the wounding pits.

A washer-woman,
hiding her bundle
under her clothes,
my wife rocks,
hands clasping
the growing mound of fate.

Child,
laundry will curtain the sun,
and your dreams be disturbed
by a damp voice crying:
"This is not my country!"

Deposed, turn your heart
to some more horizonless world
than this green wood
where the seeds fall so thickly
they would shut out the sky.

FOR EMILY RUTH

Less ugly than your brother
newborn—round, red-faced squall—
placed in my arms, you slept.

And could court that moon-time King
wherever—chair-naps, couch-naps,
cat-naps with the cats;

or lying on the playpen floor,
watching the colored birds
turn, veer on air.

But of mind indomitable.
Pushed from the edge of the bed
by your brother, you'd hoist

your small round body
back, clap your pudgy hands
and smile.

First on the backyard slide,
queen of the tire-swing,
the jungle-gym,

there was no gap too great,
no leap too far.
And from the top of the tall

maple, you'd watch the evening
train come whistling in,
and, huffing, leave the station.

May the God of the close-shut eyes
and the calm brow
be always at your beck and call—

and may the great black engine
hissing by the station platform
take you nowhere you would not go,

sweet daughter of sleep and daring.

Lounging in the green circle
of the maple-soaked sun,
where on the backs of winds
bright-shouldered with the sea,
warm clover-scent and rain
and the blue lift of horizons
the knowledge of joy so often
had come ...
                But instead he came,
waving his arms in a way
to frighten the birds, and suspend
the conversations of trees,
and stayed, and again stayed.

Crouched on the roofs of distance,
I waited, with small ears,
while his back obstructed the light
and his legs drove long shadows
over the lawn.

                But going,
he raised one light-fringed arm,
like the blade of a sword, or a hand
thrust out of water,
and I had missed once more—
through greed—
                that winged messenger.

STORY FROM ANOTHER WORLD

My father talked with ghosts—
would wake up in the pitch-black night and see
them standing there, huddled at the end of the bed—
Grandfather in his scarlet regimentals
with the little stars for wounds,
Grandmother in her Irish shawl and bonnet—
and the other dead.
"Louie," they'd whisper, "Louie, can you hear us? Listen!
We've come to tell you something. Listen, Louie—"
And sitting bolt upright
he'd talk with them
of things from another world.

And over toast and smiles we'd listen too—
to what they said and did,
to how they reached out flickering hands and touched
his cheek—just so—and to prophecies
that did not come true.

But towards the end of his life,
when he was always looking over your shoulder
out through some far-off window—
banished by rum,
or by the cancer eating in his bowels—
they became
invisible—
and waking in the pitch-dark night he'd sit
straight up—
                    listening
to his own veins beating in his ears,
the distant furnace hum, branches scraping the eaves,
but know
they were all there, standing
huddled at the end of the bed
reaching out empty hands
and whispering—
"Louie, can you hear us? Listen! We've come to tell you
something. Can you hear us, Louie? Listen, Louie,
Listen!—"

                    No one to answer them.
No one to touch.

THE SECOND DAY AFTER THE FUNERAL

Wearing my father's coat,
smudged with the fire's hands,
and on my head his cap,
I burn the weekend trash.
The pools of March, squint-eyed,
nearsighted with the wind,
reflect an older man.

Wax-paper shivers up.
The Wheaties' boxes flare—
orange breaking into life—
and sink to leprous rooms.
Newspapers eat their words.
Envelopes of letters
edge with black. Black leaves
fall upward on the air.

In dreams, last night, you held
a shaking head of tears
upon your chest—too late—,
and smiled to see the slant
road, turning, shine black.

Is it enough that now
brown, alley-ending fields,
neighbors, and the March wind
should see and not forget
the coat that binds our lives?

IN THE ROCKER

Rocking my son to sleep,
I am seized by memory—

1

Lean fingers bite
into my belly.
A grizzled cheek sands
the tip of my ear.
From one foot to the other
the dark room tilts and prances.
The mantel winks moonlight.
The clock sings three.

2

Bang! go the matchsticks shot from silver cannon.
Struck backwards
soldiers fall. It is war!
The twin lines sicken—gape.
Our flags, hung aloft, are straining.
We both cheat
to win.

3

He is the tallest man on our street.
Elm tree branches tremble
when his black hat walks.

4

Sprinting to the door
to bring my father home,
I collide with the wall.
Out of his pocket tumble the foreign countries—
blue, and carmine, and gold.
I am exultant in tears.

5

We cast off—
the sun bobs into the sky like a cut balloon.
Adrift in a path of diamonds
we bait our hooks.
My teeth chatter
so fiercely
I awaken the birds.
In the blue water
our faces are blotches of white.
The hills kindle.
The sun climbs,
and warms the encircling trees.
Philosophy falls from the sky.

Cro-Magnon
            chin
                  jutting,
jowls
      purple
and veined,
he dances the kitchen floor,
thrashing the air with his paws
and howling
impreachments and rage.

There are quarrels.
There are many quarrels.
I grow up.

We sit in the livingroom
after dinner.
He dissects the state of the nation.
I read the Sunday paper.
"The Tigers have dropped two games."
I nod from the Sunday paper.
"The Catholic Church and the Pope
are crucifying the world."

I grunt from the Sunday paper.
"There are no sons or fathers."
I read the paper.
He picks up the funnies and stares.

8

At the shop,
slumped on the edge of a bench,
(he should have retired)
his shoulders caved,
(there are taller men)
his eyes puffed and drinkshot,
(he should have retired)
he looks small.

Amidst the bustle of his peers,
bursting with overalls and pride
and medaled with lead escapes,
he is a small child
who has wandered
and been reproved.
The presses whir and howl,
consuming speech.
I tap him on the shoulder. He follows me
down the iron stairs.

. . .

From one foot to the other
the dark world tilts and prances.

I rock my son harder
and harder
to put him to sleep.

Not to rebuff the barbs,
but to hide deep wounds the child
concealed himself, ashamed,
from his father's eyes. The mind
has its shy, forbidden parts.
But the man's needs were grave
and he probed deep, cozened
by a small boy's pride.

                    Old Ghost,
I am open now to all
your hushed returns. Pity,
hatred, and fierce love stream

on the hard-packed ground that shields
you—crouched like a mocked child.

ANNIVERSARY

The beads of winter rain
hang
on my black coat
and bulged by the wind
merge in silvery mounds.
Like a soaked sponge
the earth utters pools,
and in the trees
sparrows
puff with the angers of rain.

In that far-away wood where the elms
root out the reserve of stone
how these pools
must rock his sunken sleep,
and beard with moss
the face of his dreams.

Fall down forever rain,
fall down, fall deep—

that his wood ark rise
to the dove's mountain peak.

I dreamed you were my child, and I had come
to tell you you must die. Your back was bowed,
and brittle as the wings of a dead moth
which let the light shine through. Through the late window
we watched the sun spreading in meres of haze
over the crisp September fields that crumbled,
dissolving in our glances, into gold,
and then the dark words came, and with them, tears
rolling down my cheeks, and you were the one
to comfort me—your arm about my shoulders—
and childhood's fears were all charmed away—
the kitchen floor quaking beneath black boots,
the leather strap descending (that hurt you more
than me), the tears I hid to make you sad—
and hunched together there we watched the shadows
come flocking from beneath the eaves—great bats
whose interwoven dartings blocked the sun,
and brought night down.

　　　　　　　　Let dreams invade the night
that holds you now, Father—dark voices tell you
how after many nightmares we are friends.

THE RUNNERS

Mitchell Salheeny—swift as a scythe's blade—dead.
Billy McKendricks—who swooped like a falcon, quick—
long dead.
                  John Robbins—lumbering express who always
ran
     downhill—

                  What fear you struck in our hearts—
on the playground playing tag—invincible runners.
As soon as our eyes crossed yours, the race was through—
though sidewise we spurted, zigzagged, darted and stopped,
or opened our lungs and ran till the thud of our hearts
drowned the thud of our feet pounding the close-packed gravel,
and the wire fences swam, onlookers disappeared,
and the blue sky gathered and burst.

                        Those three dark women
sit in their patience and weave. Like cunning wrestlers
they use our own strength against us.

                        Before we slow ones
have even rounded the bend you have broken the tape,
and kneel in the long blue shadows catching your breath,
though behind us still we hear you—feet thundering,
hot breath on our necks, your arms outstretched for the tag—
as if you were still here racing, your speed in the steps of the wind.

SABBATH

For Lisa, July 15, 1965

On the sun-burnt grass,
with its mummied roots
and tendrils,
on pavements through which the black tar seeps,
rooftops
curled with the sun, parched flowers,
the cracked palms of leaves
the rain falls
in sheets.

Poor shrunken earth,
how you receive it—
the dark baptism!

The ground looks up in pools—
                              Shoulders of trees
turn in a green shining—
                     Houses,
bottles, tin cans
are redeemed—
and staring through a glazed window cleansed by the rain
once more I can imagine
happiness—

           and miles away,
the room where my daughter sleeps,
just born.

MAY MADNESS

And the treetop bends in the wind, and I with the tree,
and the sky around me bends in a cloud-rich racing
of blue, and back and forth we toss with the head of the sun.

What am I doing, a man in middle age,
hugging the top of a maple where a bird might perch,
or a boy might cling, legs of his trousers swelling,
shirt sleeves flapping, sails in the moving air,
and humming aloud like a boy, or a bird, or the wind?

And below me the green fields bend, devout with May's
gold-checkered shadows, alive with swatches of sun,
and across the kneeling fields the bright wind comes,
bearing the scent, the long green drag of the sea.

And around me the rooftops sway, steeples of churches,
the far blue outlines of hills, arising, falling,
and up through the limbs of my limbs the sap of old days
streams—and I'm in love with the wind, the sun, the lifting
                                                    branches
and all things curled below—
the cat on the stoop, the woman hanging her clothes,
houses crouched intent in their wintry dreams,
and the earth in which my own roots twist and sway.

1

Weep for Philip Sousa—He is dead!
"Come quietly, John," they said,
tapping that quick-step man with his own baton,
who with a whomp of the drum dropped feet-first down
where in buttons, and braid, and honor he leads the band,
one of that underground
whose flutes are rusty with dirt,
whose piccolos wheeze,
whose horns and bassoons are pitched an octave low,
marching in double columns under the earth
while along the sides in rows
the ants all wiggle their ends,
crickets, beetles, moles
whistle the Stars and Stripes
Forever, and clapping their soundless palms
ghosts stand up and cheer.

2

I am out of step with my times—old-fashioned
and a patriot,
who from the Alaskan hills waged the Korean War,
scanning *The Nome Gazette* for Intelligence,
and before, after and since,
an optimist
fought at the hot gates,
in the salt marshes,
the Wasteland, Spengler and Doom,
while over a sinking heart and a sinking head
the headlines grow,
and who could do battle almost
for Goodness, Beauty, Truth,
if only the drums and cymbals
would thunder loudly enough,
the fifes tootle and swirl,
marching boldly, single file, down my enemies' throats
(where in the dark they lie weeping)
and tickle their ribs
with trombones.

The lions have shabbier coats
each year. More and more
they resemble Bert Lahr.
With ads and coloring books
the clowns peddle their jokes,
and over impregnable nets
queens of the high wires
dangle
        and fall—
lewd clusters of balloons.

But surely the band is of all
most beat—
the braid stripped from their coats,
striped trousers patched,
neither shoulders, hands nor feet
moving
as they play,
with incredible lack of zeal,
the sharps, flats, and rests
of the wrong notes.

Do you love a parade, dear John?
To get a parade these days
you must murder the President,
then sit for hours in black
while over confetti screens the caissons go—
Adagio, Lento, Grave.

Corelli, Torelli, Vivaldi
at double p,
they sip their whiskey sours,
staring with gloom-lit voices
over the lawns
where power-mowers whine,
dark shadows grow—
Sartre
        McLuhan
                and Dread.

Marching can be absurd.
Imagine us all stripped down—
tools of the men
thwacking their thighs in rhyme with a Scotch burr,
breasts of the women bobbing,
inflatable globes—

To procreate their kind
only birds must sing
but we—
who perch on the world's end
as on the end of an egg
and stare at the yellow stain
of misery—
what do we have to do
with trumpets,
Maestoso
and joy?

The trees are still marching, dear John,
over the hills—
and over the sun-wet fields
ranks of the wind,
and in the sky, bright-armed,
the gold-capped leader goes,
and through the rooms go I,
my children ranged behind,
mocking with clock-work limbs
and rhetorical features me—
"To the right flank, March! To the rear!"—
over tables, sofas, chairs
and upright over the walls,
our ribs resounding joy,
our feet pounding in rhyme,
while down our sweat-flushed faces
run tears—

for all of those measureless things gone down
below
that are marching still.

3

THE MESSAGE

(Dartmouth, England)

Day, day, dark day,
lowering over the roofs—
no rain in your downward hands
and face—
what message do you have for me?

The bible of fear is thumbed
to a ragged edge—all miseries
foreknown, all losses
counted up.

And yes, in the mind's reach, I know
there are suns—bronze trumpets
to open the flowers' eyes.

Would you tell me of silence speaking
into foolish ears?
Of the imprisoned heart of pearls?

Or beyond all joys and thunderings
would you intimate
how to live in the frugal shining
of this grey light?

I open the fire's door—
and bathe both neck and hands
in gusts of orange light.

The topmost coals burn blue—
chaste, unwilling ghosts—
but those far under glow
in honeycombs of heat—
constant, vermillion, sweet.

Made magical and small,
if I could live forever
in those white-cloistered rooms—

Surely the ones who turn
in endless pain,
refuse the fire's gift
and live;

and those who arise in waves
of rapt, angelic might
give their forms up and melt
into rooms of grace.

Rows of purple iris flank the walls.
Green lizards bask
on their veined tops.
The sun is a huge masseur
with golden hands.

Stretched out
on the warm faces of stones,
we are lobbing pebbles
into the shadowed niches
of walls.

Ants run over our legs
in caravans—
Bells encumber the air
with pregnant stroke—
And eleven stones in a row
go in.

From the far side of the wall there comes
a faint rustling—
hens perhaps,
combing the long, deep grass,
or a shaggy man,
feeling in the tangled shadows
for a dropped flute.

CHRISTMAS SONG

(Peace Dale, R.I.)

Sometimes in a dark frenzy I long
to heap up all I own—
books, records, furniture—
in the front yard
and strike a match.

Papers catch,
jackets of best-sellers
curdle and brown,
legs of the drop-leaf tables
kick out, roaring, lamps shatter,
paint on the Kenmore washer
bubbles
and drips—

Over the ragged tips
of oaks, flames rise,
constellations of sparks
inhabit
the air, black bodies float
upwards,
and in the heart of things appear
intolerable mangers
of snow,

where all that I never knew was mine
is born.

Hunting pebbles at the beach,
bending in the wind's path, out of reach of the waves,
and searching in the moist-grained sand for glittering stones—
milk-cloudy quartz, granite with silvery speckles,
dark-eyed obsidian— "Look!" we shout. "Come look!"
And everyone huddles around—to covet, admire, to touch—
then into our bulging pockets and on we go,
blown by the wind down the crumbling edge of the sea.

The ruff of our collie dog, swept over his collar,
gleams white as foam as he runs, entangling our legs,
sniffing the sea-wet treasures we bend to retrieve.
Down on one knee I drop—my son's shape hurtles
over my head, and soon we're all leapfrogging
over each other's shoulders and hurling pebbles,
our dearest finds, to the wind, and shouting out names—
"Emily, Sylvia, Lisa!" —and the hands that catch them
keep them, and the hands that lose them, lose them forever,
and the waves come snuffling in with long white tongues
licking at our shoes, our dog runs sidewise barking
at the waves, and on we rush down the crumbling edge of the sea.

Two miles beyond—lungs aching, fiery faces
burning like sunsets, our pockets heavy with jewels
(They will rest in pails—put away, be frittered and lost)
we turn, arms linked, heads bent, and head for home,
lurching like drunken men by the wind-drunk sea—

while the gulls overhead still circle, searching the beach
for what shy, glittering salvage, till the grey light goes.

AFTER READING WORDSWORTH'S "MICHAEL" TO HIS CHILDREN

It is all here in the room—
time, unhappiness, death—
how the cheeks of the man will age,
and wrinkle,
           how the fingers holding the book
will fumble in the yellow light
and fail,
           and the light itself fail,
and his children grow up,
and to their own children by a later light
read the same story,
or never open the book.

The boy's face turns away,
his shoulders rising, falling;
and the face of the girl looks up,
one strand of hair
glued to her shining cheeks;
and the voice of the father falters
and stops—

Never again
will they be as happy as this.
It is all here in the room—
time, misery, death—
and love,
swelling out the walls of the night
till the darkness is taken in
and the moon hangs like a lamp—
                Never again
will they be as happy as this—
as stone by stone (helped by the angel of death)
they build
the unfinished covenant.

CASUALTIES ARE AT AN ACCEPTABLE LEVEL

For Anthony Moretti

He lies on the cot
staring up.
Hats of the medics swim
through the green air.
White faces come and go.

They sprinkle the powders on
and cover up the wounds—
too wide, too deep.

Strange voices
descend from the twisted branches
of trees.

       Anthony,
goodbye.

At school well-liked,
you were one of three sons,
and did well.

Now other youngsters
are hooking the lay-ups in
behind the garage.

And over your head the branches
are filling with crows—

They are spreading their great dark wings—
They are floating
           blackly
               downwards
into your eyes.

PEACE WITH HONOR

We must not betray our manhood and accept defeat
(A paraphrase from a Nixon speech on the Viet Nam War)

It takes courage to stand
and own your mistakes.

Manhood, on the other hand,
is endless,
            cannot be proven—

Again, and again,
and again
you plunge in the flashing sword—

and all that comes back is sons,
covered with blood.

PROPERTY II

Tolstoy was right.
Whatever you own
makes you a poorer man.

They come in my dreams
and burn down house
and woods. Thieves
dig up my grass, my garden.
And even the robin's egg sky
holds lightning and storm.

All day my dog
ranges the edge of his bounds,
chasing cars, squirrels, people
to the tops of trees,
chasing the wind—
then lies in the shrubbery panting,
watching with mournful eyes
the endless procession of things,
and falls asleep and dreams
Tolstoy was right.

The sun laps at the boat.
The breeze is deep-scented with morning,
all the flowers opening their lives.

Over the gunwales I lean
and watch the bluegills hang
in the cloud-fringed depths,
or dart like thin, grey ripples
under the sky.

I have not come here to fish.
I have come to make my mind
like a still pool,
through which the clouds, the trees, the far blue hills
may glide
        softly
             as fish.

I prop my head on the thwarts and open my shirt.
The sun glows on my throat
and chest.
          It shines through my skin,
as if my whole body
were glass.

Let the boat drift
wherever the wind wills.

Every shore of the lake is dappled with light green woods!

consumes all things—
                    My father in blue coveralls,
moving across the floor to the coalbin's mouth—
the scraping of steel on cement, the thunder of coal
battering the wooden slats as the banked load shifts,
and father moving hugely with heaped-up shovel
to the mouth of the fire—not one lump spilled—and hurling
that mound of blackness in with rattle and slide—
And the flames crouching, then leaping back more fiercely,
and again my father moving across the floor
to stoke that fiery maw, gigantic-shadowed,
and the great flames' hush and roar.
                              All night red eyes
stared through the cellar's dark.

                        Bodies of men
have burned in furnaces, rising up in coils
through the blackened flues and vanishing into air
(though once three men lived there—their hands and faces
feeding on the rich substance of those fiery tongues);
and bodies of men themselves are furnaces,
where other living things are eaten, burned
into heat and light.

            Now half my life has gone.
For over eleven years the man my father
has been dead. Yet still tonight it burns, deep in the cellar
with dark insistent hum, though a different fuel,
and the flames leap up—and roar—

                        And the house is warm.

74

THE OUTSIDER

Through the black-limbed trees,
I am staring at the lighted windows of my house.

How strange they look—
lost in the tiny business
of their lives—
                all moving,
soundlessly—
                  My wife setting the plates,
my children, darting in and out
at some unruly game,
the dog prancing behind,
barking—

I watch as at some play
of mimes
(Oh the tiny figures of dreams!),
exultant, tender, sad.

On my great beast paws
I shall run to those yellow windows and hidden
peer in—

I shall wrap them in silken handkerchiefs
like dolls—

I shall sit all night in the moon,
weeping—
                weeping
for the past.

SEASCAPE

My mother and I by the sea—
my wife on the bluff's edge etching
the wind-swept waves.

The sea is performing wild feats—
hoisting the ponderous weight of its dense green body
into air, and curling over the edge of the rock-strewn shore
to thunder down in splinters, coils, eddies—

"Look at that one!" we cry, and the green sea arches hugely
over itself, lunges, breaks, and the spume
leaps skyward, sides of rocks stream white,
and under our feet
the veined foam swishes, curls—

And the wind tugs at our clothes,
lashes hair
against our wind-burned faces,
salts our lips and eyes—
and for over an hour we sit watching the waves
arch up, crumble, sweep—
drenched in the fierce green power and beauty of the sea.

Eighty times
the earth has circled the sun.
We may not come here again
                              (My mother is old,
our mother, the sea, is old),
but sit here now
happy,
lost in the thunderous burstings of the sea.

My wife stands up and waves,
her picture done.
                      We climb the bluff,
stopping at each level niche
to breathe—
and at the top
look back.

Only the moon tonight
shall see that ancient, deep-troughed face unwrinkle
and turn as smooth as a child's.

THE CLEANSING

My bathtub disapproves of all I am.
Its mind is awful,
            geometric,
                     pure.

I lie back in the waters—yellow-brown
and angular—feet absurdly propped, head cricked up
against the slanting sides—
and try to soak the wrongness from my bones.

But it is not appeased.
                      "The world is round—
The stars arranged in spirals—Infinity
one huge, white box."

                      I scour my arms and back,
and see reflected in those polished sides
my manhood floating, shriveled up and small
among the yellow suds, my knees like rocks,
barren isles, thrusting from the grey waters,
and pull the plug and watch those waters ooze
into the frothy drain—

                      And arise and scrub
my skin half raw with nubbly towels—But still
it cries:
            "Get on your knees, you filthy man, and cleanse
the dark ring from my heart!"

THE ARMOR

Tonight, though the rain beats
on the black windows
its insane tattoo,
and joints of the air burst
in gouts of thunder,
and forked lightning sees
the dark trees
flowing away like rivers
of frightened women
waving their arms,
I am too tired to care.

Fear can outmarvel fear,
and grief unman grief.

Though I knew tonight
my labors would all end
as a vast monument
to self-conceit,
and the children on whom I spend
my love and my hate
tomorrow were to cease
and turn into white lumps
of clay,
and this great ball of earth slip
through some crack in the sky
and vanish
into thin air,
I could only sit in a cold wonder
and stare
at what unlikely things
from the dark bag of possibility
can come to be.

THE EXPLORERS

Caressing each other's bodies, rapt explorers
of dearly known terrain—the slope of shoulders,
the long white curve of the back, with its minute valley,
its cloudy rising hills—hands delighting
in the sleek glide of the skin, muscled ridges
drawn taut, the clean profile of the bones—
ready for love, past ready for love, but on,
on go those hands, lost in their own volitions,
in a delirium of touch, like dancers moving
in an empty ballroom after the music's through,
as if some memory were being verified,
some blind man's landscape traced, some lost map drawn—
as if these surrendering bodies under these deft, warm
hands were melting—melting—melting like things of snow.

So here you are again
happiness—
          once more
fluttering in my half-cupped hands like a small
delicate bird
about to be freed.

That off you will loop
over the chimney tops and broomstick woods
without one backward look
is a part of joy—

And to think up reasons
why you should be—
because of the squirrels eating the sunflower seeds
on our window sill,
tails arched over their backs so twitching alive,
because of the sun poised in its three o'clock sky
so clear
there is nothing between our separate living faces
but glass,
because even now the children are coming home from school,
blowing cloud-puffs on the air, snowballing
trees, diving in drifts, and soon
the floor in the hallway will shake with the thud of their boots,
the hallway mirror shine with their burning faces—

because of the small, shy flickerings of your wings
on the underside of my hands.

THE SONG

I am bending over the fender, testing things
(pretending expertise)—
                    Inside the car
my wife is turning the ignition on
and off—
            The engine shakes, sputters,
dies—
        I disconnect the sparks
and dry the leads,
                    press down more firmly
on the distributor caps,
finger the choke, tug at the power steering belt, when suddenly,
with a dull metal roaring everything goes—My hand
streaks toward the whirling spool—There's a hot,
white flashing, and I'm holding my left hand up, one fingertip
dangling, cut to the quick, gaping like a sliced olive.
One second ago—I stare in unbelief.

The car door slams. My wife beside me screams
"My God! My God!" and runs for the phone, screaming.
I clutch my hand and stare at the welling blood,
amazed.

            In moments it seems,
I'm hunched in the front seat of my neighbor's car,
holding the finger on with a clean white hankie,
not thinking of the brown stain oozing through—
Over the railroad bridge we bounce and rattle,
and turn at the second crossing.
                        Red towers
block
        the sky.
                        . . .

On a porcelain table stretched—
On my left side the doctor's doing things—
On my right, a nurse is winding a rubber cloth
around my upper arm
and squeezing a little ball. "Be calm," she says. "Relax."
On the table top—
fingers of my right hand—drumming, drumming,
like tiny creatures moving by themselves.

"Relax," she says, in a voice from far away.
"Have you had your tetanus shot?"
I close my eyes. The fingers go on drumming.
"We'll let the nail stay on to splint the finger."
The doctor's voice. "It will come off by itself."
I lie back, distant, hidden,
while on they go—
cutting, prodding, scraping, sewing, winding—
till again those deep bass tones— "Ok there fella.
Almost as good as new. But when the shots wear off
it will really sing."
He writes on a little pad. "Take one each hour."
They help me to my feet—down the passageway
and outdoors to the car.

                     On the way back home,
we stop to get the pills. Against the hot seat cover
I lean my head, watching the bright parade
of shorts and sandals. No one glances in.
The sun shines like an ordinary day.

Back home in bed, my children ranked around,
I am a celebrity.
I speak each word, distinctly, like a little child,
and tell them of my fears that when the pain
begins, it will be too much to bear,
and over and over describe just how it happened—
how I put my hand on the power steering belt,
for no reason, how the engine roared, my hand
streaked toward that metal spool—a hot, white flashing—
my left forefinger, dangling—
and only when my own voice tires and fades,
do they rise and go.

Rigid I lie there, waiting for the pain—
thinking of how it's meant to keep the body
safe and whole, how as the Buddhists say
when attended to with your entire mind it becomes
mere fact—
            And of real suffering—
cancer patients dying in twilight wards,
the stench of flesh, white tents over labored breathings,
and all who wake in the sea-black night
and scream—

And when inside my hand the first tinglings
start, I turn on the sweating bed, my mind
fastened on those sparks that kindle, spurt and blossom
into white stalks of fire, outrageous flowers,
until my whole hand, my whole left arm is burning—
burning, throbbing, singing—

                    "I am alive! Alive!

I am alive!"

          and take the pills

                    and listen to it sing.

THE TRANSACTION

(Lynbridge, England)

I descend the steps,
          but at the street's edge
pause—
          Caught by surprise, the breadman by his truck
is turning in a slow shuffle
like a dancing bear,
and tossing from hand to hand
into the morning sun
two loaves of Wonderland—one blue,
one brown.

Into the air they spiral, wax wrappers
glittering. His face glistens with sweat. His cheeks
pucker with song, and round and around he goes
in an awkward circle, dancing,
hurling two loaves of bread
into the fresh-mint air
of early morning,
but out of one eye's corner
sees me—

          And the dance stops.
Like gravity I descend—
Goods, coins are exchanged—
and off he puffs uphill in clouds of smoke.

Like things that were never alive,
the loaves sleep in my hands.

HANDSTAND

For Lisa

After days of hurling her body
down on her hands—
and galumphing back, rear bent,
soles aching—and hours at recess
of standing against the wall
with the other girls, face down,
her coat shrouding her head
she says, "Watch this!" and runs,
throws down her hands and rises
up—back arched, her toe-tips
grazing the wall, shoves out,
and stands—
                  supremely poised.

Evolution,
what do you have to offer
beyond this?

Gulls at the window flash white wings
and squeal applause.

I smack her on the rear,
and down she tumbles,
giggling on the floor.

THE INFLUENCE

For Sylvia

Like a green shoot, under the topsoil, thrusting
up—
    making the moist, black earth-clods
tremble and heave—
        you are always
there.

I am thinking my separate thoughts,
engrossed in the business of the day—
buying bread at the baker's, paying the electric bill,
hunting for washers at the hardware—
but always under the mind's
surface
    that green trembling—

How happy the smell of the bread!
The dime glows in my hand!
I walk down sun-glazed streets that ripple like seas of flowers!

—On a hill of sheep, crouched down like two black stones,
fooling the clouds that wander over the rim
of the blue May sky, wooly and slow as sheep,
but not the sheep—the small-brained, foolish sheep—
who know where black stones sit, and drift uphill,
calling their young with broken, nasal baas,
who answer in higher keys and trot stiff-legged
to their mothers' sides and kneeling under one flank
thrust up ferociously—clearing the dug—
and tails waggling in a wooly frenzy, drink—

Warm barnyard smells—The May sun drowzing down
upon our necks and shoulders. Like stones we sit,
watching the clouds slow-drifting over the hills,
lazy as sheep.
                    Against the green-wool curve
of the hill, how whitely the young lambs shine as they frisk
in idiot loops of joy. Two come so close
we could almost reach a hand and touch their soft,
mischievous faces.
                    But stones don't move, and today,
in this warm May sun we are content to be
like stones—like sheep—like barely drifting clouds.

Wind turbans round their heads.
Wrap them in red-gold robes.
Prophets—patriarchs—you with the downward smile
and thin moustache, Joseph, go home! Even now
your father's stretching out his trembling hands
over the heads of your sons.
And you with the shifty glance and evasive eye, Peter,
don't turn away! The policeman's listening.
We know your after-life.

Ahead a woman in tight-sheathed skirt is mincing
on pigeon-toes—the round halves of her rear
bobbing up
and down.
She stops at a jeweler's window. There in the glass
her blond face, mirrored, glows. Diamonds, emeralds
pour through her dimpled hands.
                                    Saskia, beware
of those sensual glitterings! One year
and you're dead!

The couple on the bus get up to go.
Lightly on her shoulder he rests one hand;
the other open-palmed across her chest
with a shy tenderness.
                          Light through their bodies
streams—

          O people of Amsterdam—
you at the window, woman with the small pink flower,
child in the courtyard leaning on your broom,
bankers, lawyers, doctors, merchants, deadmen—
you are all saved,
glowing on velvet walls in fine-lit rooms
in blacks, ambers,
golds—

          Like a great white cloud, compassion
floats over Amsterdam.

4

CHECKMATE

I am playing chess with my daughter.
The end is near.
Blackly arrayed, my powers are sweeping in
for the last assault.
Under my breath,
I'm humming Christmas carols,
and drumming the table top with my fingertips,
when glancing casually up—
I see her face.

And my mouth turns dry, hands turn heavy as lead, my eyes
strain—
          searching the checkered spaces, up and down,
endlessly—

          Beside the board, huddled like sheep,
stand the dead—
                    tall, lonely, white.
Each move is the fatal move, each touch the end.
And when at last bishop and queen close in
I'm almost glad.
The pain is through.
There is nothing more to fear.
Checkmate!

And misery sweeps over me in waves—
for all the coming losses of her life.

THE TRUST

Because all things are melting
into other things,
we walk through the dark house shyly,
touching with naked fingers,
those hidden forms,
those dim, courageous shapes,
fixed tremblings—
grainy backs of chairs,
the cool, glass throats of vases,
the stems of lamps—
and touching with aching fingers
the shapes of each other's lives.

Your breasts lie in my hands
like glowing pools,
pressing softly downwards—
but there is no time—no time
for passion. Everything must be touched!
Everything in the house!

Even now those shapes are fading,
like the voices of whippoorwills—

Snow from the branches,
stripped—ice-glitterings—
the jewelled tiara of twigs—

Once more the trees stand bare,
black-rutted trunks
looming, a crisscross tangle of heads.

Bushes beside the road,
like whips unstrung,
pools in the fields, brown-faced,

the ground frizzled with tufts—
I am not immune
to wintry theatricals,

the white descensions of clouds,
or the slow, upward pushing
of shoots.

But now in this nameless season
rest content
with the starched backgrounds of things—

grainy pavements of roads,
black earthen wounds,
the caked refuse of leaves,

and the way the light falls strictly
on houses, faces, woods
and will not lie.

One light in the room—arched dimly
over her head—

As over a child's cradle she bends,
her hands
feeding the cloth in smoothly.

Her neck strains. The wrinkles in her skin
shine out in ridges and troughs. Her eyes blink—

The needle goes stammering in,
the stitches march
down the broad face of the cloth
and the spools unwind;
and over this luminous hollow of light
night
      bends
            like a cave.

Suspended from time,
the picture might seem complete;
but soon the stammering will cease,
                  the needle hang
motionless on air,
          and my mother rise,
snap off the sewing light,
and move through the cumbrous darkness
to bed.

THE ACCOUNTING

1

The sky opens its sluices—The rain pours down.
Through an underwater world—green-wavery, dim—
where nothing has clear form or shape we're moving.
The flip-flop of the windshield-wiper's blades
clears only a moment's glance—dark, thrashing trees
bent over small white houses, red-glazed barns
dissolving to crooked streams. In the far lane,
the yellow eyes of cars swell out and pass
in misty geysers. The rain rattles and thumps.
We pull off onto the shoulder of the road
and sit there, hushed, our faces silvery blobs,
listening to the downpour of the rain.

2

It has not come, wisdom. One decade from death,
and all my truths have wandered back to questions,
within whose bending sickle heads I live,
the fool of experience, anxiety's saint.
It has not come, goodness—Heaven leaping down
in a transport of light—a sudden shifting of names
and identities. (I must die myself, my faults
all heaped upon me, made heavier by age.)
Winds stalk the hills, the sea lunges in its den,
deep in its burrow, the animal crouches shivering.
Once one of God's chosen ones, I have become
a man with a curious mission—to live until I die.

3

Body, I have dwelt too long in this hovel—
cheap tenement with the sagging walls, loose paint
dangling from ceilings, holes in the plaster,
cracks beneath the doors, through which the wind
blows with a bitter wailing—

              And in this mind
too long—home movie that repeats itself in dreams
and memories, sad phonograph of hopes and fears,
now slowly winding down—And as for you,
small dwarf with the outsized hands, envy-master, pimp
with the street-wise glance and pocket full of knives,
go pound on some other door. I am not at home
to your wheedlings. There is some better world!

4

Nightmares stalk the city. I recognize
those grotesque shapes—How have you left my mind
imaginings, dark fantasies, frenzied dreams?
Are there cameras behind my eyes? Newspapers eavesdropping
on my sleep? Black masses of moving bodies
march across the faces of the dead and dying.
One lean cadaver rises, grasps one leg
and strips it of its meat. The air grows rich
with internecine clouds. Rats tend the poor.
Streams foul the rivers, black rivers foul the seas.
Earth bubbles up with the ooze of poisoned springs.
Violins play on the veins of dried-up moons.

5

In the long passage of night there comes a time
when the pictures of the past that whine and flicker
on the screen, and the past that's yet to be,
are stilled, and like a mist rising from a lake,
you float above your bed with its tangled sheets,
and look down at the curled shape of your life.
How tiny it all seems—ambitions, hopes, fears,
this body's slowly dissolving aches and joys,
this world and its slowly crumbling histories—
all cradled in the white curve of a smile.
And buoyed up by the soft night air you drift
outside to sing with the crickets in the fields.

6

Twilight is a good place—white houses fading
into darkening woods—trees melting to trees.
Slowly the mirror purges its images,
and from that chastened glass swims up a face
which sheds no images, and in your ears
a voice which is no voice—"Dear little being,
to cling to these melting forms is joy, is grief,
is being alive. It is all meaningless,
all full of meaning. The stars burn in their shrouds.
Mountains walk barefooted to the sea.
Now and forever are one. Be a happy moment!
Give up your pride—Come, dance within my hands."

Part of my nose has gone before I go.
Where are you now, right nostril—sniffing the air
of nowhere, aromas of the past, bright worlds
beyond?

But they'd all like to be gone—
the right foot and the left foot plant new footprints
down other paths,
hands take another hold,
mind, body, heart
disperse, depart.

Born travelers, they would like to see the world,
be some other person, parts of some other whole,
someone better, worse,
try a new planet, some far-off universe—
in short, be off, be gone.

Some morning I will wake in bed, alone,
invisible—
                a man of delinquent parts—
rise up and meet the sun—
myself, no body, no one,
and walk through the morning air like a clear, bright window
so—-

        and follow my nose
and go.

WINTERBERRY

(A Celebration of Retirement After 31 Years of Teaching)

Long strings of scarlet berries jewel the snow,
summer's fruits, startling the bedded white.
All things reborn—all changed, transformed, new-made!
Bushes like ghosts, crouched down, about to rise.
Paths freed from old directions, rutted roads—
The ground itself waiting for someone's footprints
to tell where the ground might be—Margins, margins
how you delight my eyes! And you, red berries,
that make white margins sweet and bring the birds.

Winter, for all your winds and zero ways,
I am a collector of your white and scarlet fruits,
your red-barred sunsets, your linen-hooded hills.

Amazing, that I've grown so young so old!
almost to begin again—this blue-veined hand,
mottled with liver spots, crisscrossed with age,
the hand to write the new book of my life.

Three children grown, and countless children stored
in worn green ledgers (the savings of thirty years),
and time, free time, heaped on me from the past,
I have forgotten the names of days. One Sunday stretches
before me and behind. The calendar
shuffles its many months. The clock's hands move
quick-paced or leaden-slow as I prescribe.
I rise when I wake. I go to sleep when I will;
or stay up half the night to watch the moon
accomplish its clear, white circuit of the sky.
And in the morning, all of heaven's birds
fly down at my coming forth, alight and feed.

I am the apprentice and the master of my days!
None but the wind commands my moving hours!
(Though sickness and pain wait by the opening door.)

I shall go outside and walk in the fallen snow,
striding back and forth, through drifted mounds and valleys,
making pathways, leading nowhere, and everywhere.

I shall build upon the lawn a huge white snowman
with broomstick arms, and a winterberry smile.

AIR SICKNESS

The plane's nose lifts, and up my mother goes
into white-bellied clouds—and vanishes—
Ninety-six years carried to some heavenly home.

Relieved of the wheelchair's weight, the diapers' stench,
the nagging whistle that nightly blew and blew,
our spirits soar.

But sink with the dull nostalgias of goodbye—
the common ache of farewell—this time perhaps
the last—

And soar with dappled, rhododendron lawns,
unfettered rooms—and books, and friends, and music—

And sink with the thought of that far-off nursing home,
and the nurse who left her in her wheelchair half one night
to teach her never, never to get up alone.

And soar because we did it—kept her alive
for one month more, two pounds the better,
and not one single fall—

And sink because so soon we'll be like her—
our children watching as the plane's nose rises slowly
into the clouds—relieved, elated, sad.

And sink, and soar, and sink till the stomach rolls
with so many risings, fallings—

                              In such a storm
of vexed, contrary feelings, wind-baffling winds,
how can any traveler reach his goal;
any plane
          fly true?

WINTER ROBBERY

Like exotic birds,
fourteen robins light
on my winterberry,
orange breasts against the snow's
deep-bedded sheen, and peck
the fruit.

One by one those clear
red globes wink out
and vanish, small scarlet fires
which lit up winter's grey
so cheerily.

I run out waving my arms,
and they wheel up, scatter, perch
in the tops of trees.
But before the front door
shuts, swoop down and eat.

Again I run out, shouting,
clapping my hands, and again
they explode in a torn fluttering
of wings—alight and wait.

The bushes are being stripped—
fruits red dots, too sparse,
too Japanese.

I plot and act like God.

All afternoon a man
with an orange cap and a wire
body, stands in the snow,
and, broomstick arms outstretched,
wards off the birds.

Till their black-winged shadows rise,
skirting the trees,
I watch, I wait.

The few red berries left,
against the deep drifts burn
like drops of blood.

And so the door swings shut—
and hunched down foolishly,
one cheek against the cold,
enameled wood, we catch
the sound of steps—retreating
(or is it only the big
veins throbbing in our heads,
the soft thud of tears?),
and crouch half through the night,
pressing the smooth molding
against our cheeks and saying
small things into the cracks;
like children sent to bed
from their own birthday party—
all of their best friends there.

THE ALTERATIONS

I must distance myself from these small alterations
they're making in this body I'm living in.
No part of me—these gnarled fists of aches,
these feet that walk on tiny, naked pins.
The house is not my house—I'm merely renting—
and the lease sets forth the terms in the plainest way.
Still, after spending a lifetime in one place,
you come to feel at home, the house seems yours
and the alterations vex you—always downwards,
always for the worse. The front door creaks and groans,
the plumbing fails, the swollen windows stick,
and from beneath the floors come rumblings—
faint warnings to prepare you for that day
you know will come yet never quite believe,
when back from work one dusk you'll find a sign
propped on the lawn, *For Sale*, and try your key
in the front door, and discover the lock's been changed,
and stand there, on your own front porch, a stranger,
feeling outraged, grieved, yet somehow in the wrong—
and turn away.

      Surely there are other lodgings
somewhere—accomodations in lands where you've never been.

The blackbirds are hungry. They are rattling the trees like doors,
congregating on lawns in flocks, like black-cloaked believers,
bending bushes down, making criss-cross paths of the air.

I take out baskets of sunflower seeds and fill the feeders,
lay suet in great white slabs on the window tray,
replenish the birdbath with fresh, clear coils of water—

but almost before I'm through and back inside
the seeds are white husks on the ground, the shelf is bare,
the water shaken out in wing-drops, the birdbath dry.

I step on the porch and address them, like some public informer,
and tell them where the starving are, where the old ones lie,
coordinates of the most disastrous wars,

and they fly off in clouds, darkening the air for days,
dragging night from the bushes and trees. The sound of their
                                                    wing-beats
haunts the roofs of sleep like the sound of wind-driven rain.

But three stay back. They perch on my window sill—
three gold-ringed eyes, staring in—staring in—and wait.
Good scavengers, they can sense the smell of decay.

It's their business to strip the dark, decaying tissue,
to peck from the loaves of the brain dead memories,
scour the odors off and render the white bones clean.

"Have mercy!" I plead. "Be swift! You are guests! You are guests!"
But they know too well, like any skillful workers,
when the time is right, and when it is not quite time.

And only at moments do I feel the probe of their beaks
in my lungs, my heart, the scrape of their claws on my skull—
as downwards I move, towards that body which is not yet me.

DEATH, DARK SHADOW, WALK

Death, dark shadow, walk
always by my side.
In your clear shade all living things
are purified.

Gold-rich, the moving sun—
Quick-green, the gliding trees—
As swift as jewels the birds that dart
among the leaves—

And every face that passes,
haloed by that dark light,
shines out with a rich, dissolving shine
like lamps at night—

And body, poor compendium
of curious aches and pains,
takes on a grace, like weathered stone
washed by the rains.

Greed—envy—hatred—lust
melt in that scrutiny,
and the good shines clear, as in the light
of eternity.

Stay near me, guardian shadow.
Be that winged one heaven sends—
until the night falls, and in that darkness
all darkness ends.

Strange gravity—that, as I grow
downwards, toward the earth,
loosens those fingers, one by one,
which bound me from my birth.

Attractions of light diminish, birds
sing in ambiguous keys.
Red flowers close. The moon sinks down
behind black-netted trees.

What but some huger, darker planet
swimming out of the night
could break this ancient spell and wean me
from this green world of light?

And the light beckons—and light is all.
Far down beneath you, the body lies,
lost in its hopeless miseries,
that heavy body which is not you.

How small the pain-clenched face, how small
the tired hands, the granite feet,
weighed down by all that gravity—
though the light beckons, and light is all.

Stop the mourners' tears before they fall—
Silence the grown-up children's cries,
as upwards, into the light, you float
from this heavy body which is not you.

Earth shrinks into a minute ball,
so far down under, you cannot see
where the sun in that void of shining dies—
and the light beckons, and light is all.

How strange, that our fondest hopes come true!
That when from these flesh-bound shapes we rise
it is all freedom—no me, no you—
and the light beckons—and light is all.

—who even as the bud unsheathed
felt the flower wither in the leaf,
and eyeing the ever-burning stars
saw night close in and quench their fires,

let these last words he set to rhyme
lament the loss of loss and time,
then quiet take that tongue, that pen
here where all elegies have an end.

II.

PORTRAITS, HISTORIES AND MYTHOLOGIES

THE OLD POET LOOKS AT THE NIGHT SKY

When I was young, watching this same moon, huge,
rise through the gap-toothed houses in the east,
and hearing the March wind wrestling the black-topped elms
till their branches scraped the eaves, I dreamed the power
that lived in that moving darkness lived in me.

Now, having done all that I could, and failed,
I am content tonight to feel it still,
out there, moving through the barren, moon-tossed branches,
and know when I am dead it shall live on,
though not in me—having served it with my life.

THE SERVANT

Plants in every window of the house—
green mouths on tiptoe crying
in their leafy tongues.

Each morning, the ritual—
the long-nosed watering can
tipped over small clay pots,
the round clear ropes of water dangling down
to feed dark roots.

Watered too much,
the leaves turn brown
and fall.
Watered too little, the leaves turn brown
and fall.

Light favors the bedroom windows to the south.
I move them back and forth
between the rooms,
before the long stems droop,
the querulous voices hush and fade
to whispers.

The punishment for negligence
is death—limp bodies thrust
in the trash can,
or tucked under matted weeds in the vacant lot—
where they may go on crying
years.

        They devour
my days.

Sometimes I long to sweep the windows clear
of that green clutter—that labyrinthine
growth—
                and be free.

But nurturing is my life.
I am the servant of plants.
Light shining through green foliage makes me glad.

REMISSION

"To release, relax, refrain—postpone
for a period—as with the symptoms of a disease."

She stood by the kitchen counter staring out
at the uncut lawn, watching the cowbirds stalk
through the long deep grass, heads poised like dinosaurs.

Through the oaktrees' branches, the morning sun cast plots
of jagged light. The dandelions blazed
in their furry hundreds. From branch to branch
blue jays fluttered, crying their raucous cries—
It was all as it should have been, yet somehow changed.

Just six weeks back—at this same time of day—
the telephone had jangled—breaking the quiet
air with its anxious ring. She had lifted the receiver—
listened to words, humming along distant wires—
and into his veins those deadly cells had swarmed.

She could close her eyes and see them—slim, grey shadows
gliding along the dark streams of the blood,
eating the good cells swimming in shoals before them.

To remit, relax, postpone for a period—
remission of debts, remission of sins, remission—

An even or better chance, the doctors said,
caught at an early stage, a lesser strain.

He was the oldest patient on the children's ward,
the doctors' and nurses' favorite. He joked with them,
and entertained the visitors with skits
and pantomimes, putting them at their ease.

Cross-legged on the bed, he took her hands,
as if he were the parent, she the child.
"Together we're going to lick this thing, you'll see,
you and I and Dad and all our friends.
Did you ever dream we had so many friends?"

They had been kind. The kitchen counter still
was heaped with cakes and pies. The refrigerator
stuffed with meat loaf, jello salad, fruit.
There were not so many errands in the week
as had been spoken for. In every drive
a car stood poised. The phone was off the hook
from so much sympathy. They had been kind.
The drugs would work. He would get well. And yet—

Under her thoughts always those slim, grey shadows
swarmed, devouring hope, mocking her prayers
and making a restless nightmare of her dreams.

This sun—which shone so bravely on the leaves
had shone as bravely then, just six weeks back
when he was well, and would shine down as bravely
upon some future day—linked lines of cars,
curling in slow procession up the hill,
through stone gates into a wood of stone.

To relent, relax, postpone for a time—remission—
but never the end of nightmare, each day waking
to that vague sense of dread which would not vanish
however brightly the sun might choose to shine,
however busily she kept her hands
moving, her mind on other thoughts—remission—
but never the end of nightmare or of fear.

As a girl in high school she had read somewhere
that life itself was only a brief remission
between one dark and another, later dark—
and no doubt it was so. The young interns,
doctors who talked so wisely of disease,
the nurses who treated each child as their own,
in their veins too the dark marauders swarmed—
awaiting their cue—the turning of a leaf.
Whatever was living, breathing in the world
stood poised on the brink of death!

                                      Which brought no comfort.
The time was now, and this life was her son's.

Breakfast through, she'd clear away the dishes,
bake him his favorite date loaf and a pie,
and take them up that afternoon and say
how well that he was looking (He did look well),
how soon he'd be going back to school (He would),
and how together with the prayers of friends
they'd lick this thing and he'd get well—Oh yes,
dear God, he would get well, he would—

If only those slim, grey shadows would slink back
into their holes—If only the morning sun
would shine less lavishly on the green-palmed leaves—
blue jays stop their anxious flutterings
from branch to branch—If only he wouldn't die—

THE REVENANT

For Peter Findlay

Like a hummingbird among rich summer flowers,
your ghost appears—
bright-flashing, flicker-sudden, and as brief
as your brief life—
and after so many years
brings back the joy you gave us—the love—the grief,
as if the years were hours.

Summer-swift your days, three winters long your dying,
and with such pain;
but with each year your spirit grew more strong,
more loving-tongued,
till loss half turned to gain,
and you, the young, seemed old, and we, the young,
and the dying taught the living.

So back you dart, not as some sad earth-haunter
but as this bird,
this brilliant apparition that haunts the rooms
of rich perfumes,
whose voice is seen, not heard—
singing of a garden of sweeter, rarer blooms,
blooming in some greater summer.

THE OLD PRO'S LAMENT

Each year the court expands,
the net moves back, the ball
hums by—with more spin.

I use my second serve,
lob deeper, slice more,
stay away from the net, and fail
to win.

As any fool can tell
it is time
to play the game purely
for the game's sake—to applaud
the puff of white chalk,
shake hands
and grin.

Others retire
into the warm corners of memory,
invent new rules, new games
and win.

Under the hot lances
of the shower, I play each point over,
and over,
and over
again.

Wisdom is the natural business
of old men—
to let the body go,
the rafters, moth-eaten and decayed,
cave in.

But nightly in dreams I see
an old man
playing in an empty court
under the dim floodlights
of the moon
with a racket gone in the strings—
no net, no ball, no game—
and still playing
to win.

ALZHEIMER'S

Under her face
some stranger has set up house,
and locked the doors.

But the doorknobs rattle, hinges
bend— "George, George," she shouts
and is back.

Sharp things put up,
cards on half the objects of the house
naming their proper names,
she sits with crinkled brow
over her children's books,
fingers tracing the words—
or at the breakfast table
rolling her ring,
again, and again, and again,
over the table's edge
into her lap.

I dream of her death—
white skeleton trees
in a wintry swamp
in the calm dignities of cold—

"Cut your losses," they say.
"Shut her up," they say.
"If you could imagine half the things
to come—"

I imagine them—
Tooth-marks on my hands,
the restraining straps,
diapers, bib, the dark, unknowing eyes—

(Day by day, she is injuring
memory—
Forty years of love
rolled like a stone on my back,
which must be rolled off now
as if from the mouth
of a grave.)

Only at night can I stand
looking down at that face
returned to itself by sleep,
and caress, again and again,
not touching the skin,
the hollows under the eyes,
the curve of the cheek,
the white pinched forehead—

and whispering under my breath
dreams, prayers, childish longings—
that will not be met.

She was not no one.

She had a given name,
a drawer of knitted things,
matched suits and sweaters,
a crib under the window
where the sun could look.

"Others will come," they said,
"to take her place."
                (And they did.)
"Lucky," they said, "it happened now,
  before ..."
            (And it was true.)

Nine swelling moons,
like a small Greek goddess,
she ruled my moods,
talking in a morse code
of thumps and kicks.

But born still-born she was hustled
faceless away
to save a mother's
grief.

Foolish to mourn for someone
who was so nearly no one,
and after five long years grieve
still
      though less and less.

Possibility
is not fact.
What never came to be—
never was.

(Though half the world's mourning
is for what never
was.)

Still, it was an error
not to take that tiny shriveled body
in my arms,
not to touch that thin, clenched face.

A grief that has no shape
is imageless.

Like a hidden fish it swims
under the sea, surfacing
at will,
or like a dark moon peers
through the window of any season,
any mood.

A grief without a shape
is endless.

It has no grave.

I saw him then—suspended by his pain
between two spheres of dark and lost to each;
himself a face his memory could not reach;
the world a streetlight guttering in his brain.
Time grew on him, and through his mouth decay
exhaled its acrid loss; I heard that speech.
I saw the walls close in, the light turn grey,
and cold mount up the granite limbs to death.
I breathed with him his last foul-taken breath;
and in his death the world was cleansed away.

Through a looking-glass of tears I saw those lands
I knew but never saw: September trees
so eloquent with green, unfallen leaves;
that slanting autumn sun that cups the hands;
old men upon the evening steps, so fair
they hurt the eyes; birds, blue tragedies
plunging down the gold-embodied air.
Even the factory bricks were bright with loss,
and every street shone golden and wore a cross.
I was alive and beautiful with care.

Father, it was not good. I will not make
the follies of your pain, your poor, tricked mind
deceits of sly magicians who are kind.
This world is not a world to give or take,
and death has no forgiveness from the blind.
But in that second's love your losing gave
I saw a land no living thing may leave;
and lost to what I was, my senseless world,
I lived by right of suffering in that world
before I too slipped back into the grave.

PEGASUS: A COMEDY IN EIGHT SCENES

I

He threw his bat down third and seized the pen:
"My words will make the ages, gentlemen!"

II

"To say the sun direct!" They clanked their beers,
and heard their stomachs cry, the angels cheer.

III

Even his dog disliked it. "Trite! Amen."
He wept and ate the lions in his den.

IV

"Have you read Mr. Cambry? You hadn't heard!
He flapped his wings one day and was a bird."

V

"And now, in this falling age?" "The world will last."
"He's right! He's right!" He couldn't. The world went past.

VI

"Once upon, a poet went to words."
Some small songs came—Perfection. It was absurd.

VII

His final statement came out on a stone:
"I fought with time and now it holds its own."

VIII

The rhymes went mad; the diction strange. "My dear!"
The ages wept and dropped him like a tear.

Small cock of the walk—
bright-plumaged at eighty-three—
she rules the roost.

Her daughters cower
under the brisk loquations of her tongue
(remembered tyrannies).

"How marvellous," we say.
"How full of life!"

Nothing's too minute—
from the time it takes to cook the Sunday meal,
to the interrogation of her granddaughters' suitors
in the living room, all's overseen.

And when (as always) she talks about the past,
the past is now.

       Brown ghost of thirty years,
out of the locket round her neck he steps—
each tone of voice, each trick of speech
known more familiarly
than our favorite characters
on television.

      "One day," she says,
we'll be rejoined in Heaven."
(The angels squawk like hens,
hiding their heads in their wings.)

Death, cunning fox,
when into the barnyard of this world you slink
in search of prey,
      be cautious whom you take
into the velvet quiet of your house.

She cut through things—her face
like a knife's blade, voice
both clear and sharp.

She told the man she married that if love
were a will to children, an appreciation
of sex, a fear of loneliness,
she loved him.

          Fall nights
she'd lie awake listening to the wind outdoors
raking the leaves from gnarled, frost-rimed branches,
and mock the shiver of joy that coursed her back.

Children she loved
and cats.
          She brought them up
to be themselves, speak truth, and lie
only when necessary.

Her mirror never lied.
She smiled at the skeleton behind the mask
growing serenely out,
who smiled back.

Though all her friends appreciated her rare candor,
they kept it for rare occasions.

Monthly her husband confessed
indiscretions which as he said
"she would wish to know."

Her children grew up.

She took it all—without self-pity, recriminations,
or regret—
          but with one fear—
the bruised fruit of the world sliced to the core,
what if she found
no clean stone at the heart?

Back in the house of their lives
what most surprised him was how of all these things
they had invested with so many years
of joy and suffering
                nothing spoke.

Even her ashes hid
in the pewter urn behind the cupboard door
were still. "Strew them," she'd said
"beside the brook in back of the willow grove
where I and the children played."
                        But going there,
he found the farm in strangers' hands, the willows
chopped down at the roots, the stream black-faced
and slow,
              and brought her ashes home.

The March wind spoke,
hurling late wings of white against the walls,
its brutish whine rising to a howl.

Six times the hammers thudded in her heart.
She dropped the saucer, sank back in the chair,
surprise moving across her face like a blank,
white sheet.

              Evicted from the room, small boy
who couldn't hold his sorrows in, he paced
the hall, stopping five times to hear her breathing stop,
faint whisperings, answering the doctor's voice
(but not to ask for him, or say goodbye),
and then the door opened, and she was gone.

After their first child died, the doctor said
it wasn't safe to have the other four;
but in the country children grow up strong
and tall—
              The voice of his daughter, rising to a wail—
"You were not the marrying kind. You should have lived
single, without children. You'll not come now
to our house and do to our three daughters
what you did to us."

Quarrels—there had been quarrels—
and always the damning words it seemed were his,
her silence moving behind those peevish thunders
in perfect argument.

          And now this final silence
that answered everything.

              The March wind wailed,
lashing the clapboard walls until it seemed
the slant, red roof would flap its wings and fly;
but inside—only silence.

            He longed to go
and do a crazy thing—open the closet door,
lift the urn down from the topmost cupboard shelf,
and moving through the rooms shake out the ashes
into this quiet air—until her dust
covered everything—rugs, furniture, floors—
with its own fine powder, but only sat there,
hunched in the brooding darkness like a toad,
hearing the wind lashing the bat-winged trees.

She lowers her body in and pushes off,
cold surging against her neck and shoulders
as she heads straight out, cleaving the pond's smooth face,
and leaving behind a path of bubbled light,
(Pines by the cabin shrink, the dock grows small)—
and leaving behind these last few months of pain
and misery—the white-draped cubicle, the harsh,
carbolic smell, love's shrunken head afloat
on its hollow pillow, eyes gummed shut,
mouth a cave round which a red tongue roves
like a frantic animal, searching for meanings lost
in that scooped-out dark, that cancer-eaten world—
and leaving behind the guilt of being well,
sad gravities of sleepless nights, dull fears,
nightmares, and the weight of her own body
which one day will betray the life it feeds
to this same numb dishonor and decay.

The sun flakes from her arms and warms her neck.
Halfway across, she turns upon her back
and swims with a lazy stroke, the spring-fed dark
beneath, above, the sky's blue grotto
in which she is also floating, beside white clouds—
the warm good wooly clouds, tinctured with sunlight—
weightless, desireless, consumed by a happiness
too deep for any purpose, any name,
her limbs lifting with the gently lifting waters,
the blue and easy motions of the sky—
all memories lost but the memories of now.

But slowly, behind her head, the hills loom up—
the prickly-headed pines, the white-trunked birches—
and not reaching down to touch the oozy depths
she turns, and begins to swim the long way back.

IN THE TOWER

(For the Earl of Warwick, imprisoned as
a child, executed in early manhood.)

The room, like this, was cold.
You read to yourself, wrote letters,
played cribbage with your keeper,
and from that grated window on special days
watched the executions—heads
toppling from the block.

At seventeen years, a stutterer
with a shifty eye, once a week
they let you take the air,
walking these battlements,
watching the lions roar
in the pits below.

Succession forced the King's
hand. A plot was devised
sufficient for the dull-witted,
and up you went,
kicking to the gates of heaven,
a headless angel.

Now tourists throng this dark and musty room.
"We have come to save you,
my Lord."
             But no one's here.

In a room without doors,
far off in the perfect prison
of history, you lie—small boy,
biting your nails,
watching for dawn,
listening for soldiers' steps upon the stairs.

And so again it seems that human pain
may be a devious thing, and all our fears
    so many hidden doors
    into the appointed place.

From islands—wind-tossed hills riding the sea—
you moved into the quarried bins of shame,
    and lost—yourself,
    your family, an entire past—

And like a one-legged man stumped down the streets,
owned by the subtle wanderings of that maze,
    finding in each face
    marks of the storied beast.

And grew, until that nightmare city seemed
the whole God-given world, and suffering
    too deeply yours to share
    or, grieving, give away.

Then cloud-like rose, into the evening sky,
and huge with the borrowed weight of all you were
    rained a child's joy
    on the green hill of the world.

rises before the sun.

Just as the first mists lift from the steaming lake
he wades
into ice-blue waters,
                    baptizing
the day.

He breakfasts on wind and birdsong—
breathes in the hidden planets of the air—
hoes beans.

Whatever needs dusting, the mind
undusted still,
he throws away.

But possesses
everything—
orchards, wheat fields, barns, dark acres of trees—
one glance
and they're his.

Under the green-gold shadows of rustling grain,
ripe grape clusters, he discovers—
a new life.

And crouches hours on his knees
recording the Trojan Wars, the Iliad
of ants.

He unfathoms springs of ponds, eats woodchucks raw,
fishes in the stream of time for eternity,
and when the red-faced sun (that morning star)
sinks behind black hills
he lies in the dark of his own head marvelling
at the inventions
of dreams—
                    and teaching the night owls
psalms.

KINDERTOTEN

For Sigmund Freud

"He told me afterward that his loss had affected him in a different
way from any of the others he had suffered. They had brought
about sheer pain, but this one had killed something in him for
good. ... he said that Heinerle had stood to him for all children
and grandchildren."

Jones, The Life of Sigmund Freud

After the death of children, something died;
and for the first time, and the last, came tears.

Feeling down dark tunnels on hands and knees
and turning the last bend, his heart drained
of blood, he had stared at that cavity
from which all legend comes, and all nightmare,
and had not turned his head.

              And afterwards,
as cancer ate his lower face away
in thirty-three slow mouthfuls, and the dark
thoughts of the head descended into the mouth
as smell and taste, he had not breathed a word,
or cried out.

            But in the child's body
there must have been much hidden—many loves
and small, lost things—to make that man of truth
not only turn his head away, but water,
like some blind king, the dark roots of the world.

AFTER THE EXPULSION

Light as a figment of belief
the garden left their memories.
The world outside seemed formed to please,
and there were anodynes for grief.

At first, in strange, incendiary skies,
they watched the sun give up its heat,
and felt beneath their naked feet
the grass blades shrivel up and die,

and in the woman's swelling girth
the dream of death approach, the snake,
and afterwards, the threatened ache
of loss covering the entire earth.

But year stalked year, and summer's leaves
still wore their faultless summer hues,
in spite of autumn's colored ruse
and the white coat that winter weaves.

The light-winged ones had fled, but fled
just one tree over, perched and sung,
and over the sheer-faced hill still hung
that lucid disc, that matchless head.

And then the quarrel—outrage—cries—
and blood to water the desert's root.
And they remembered the garden's fruit,
and which green side was Paradise.

THE FLOOD

After the eighth day, fear
must have come flooding in
with the brown trickle of water
under the door—the crops
drowned, hams from the cellar
dangling from the beams,
and all tired
of the coziness, the games.

And as the waters
rose—to window height—
and there was no land left,
even inside, and chairs,
buckets, tables
began to lift, and swim,
they must have sensed something
incredible—the end of a world.

And from the rooftops, rain
thudding on their bent heads
washing their bodies clean
of hope, their children
moaning with hunger and cold,
what strange sights—birds
dropping from the branches of trees
like fruit, dull-winged.

Inside the ark, meanwhile,
the thunderous volleys of rain,
bawling of cattle, bedlam
of dogs, hyenas, wolves,
and their own children's cries
would have hidden the sound of fists
pounding on the wooden hull—
those few survivors left,
clinging to the one island
before adventuring down
to join the rest of the world.

And afterwards, when only rain
was heard, creaking timbers,
the buck and slap of waves,
how hard it must have seemed—
to be among those chosen
to float, perhaps forever,
on the terrible angers of God;
or land after many days
on some bare mountain top
and blinking in the harsh light
emerge—the same men—
to begin a better world.

Unlike that famous singer, she believed.
Angels had been her guests
and struck the eyes of men
blind.

She turned—to see His face,
towering behind the dense
columns of fire, enraged
and beautiful;

or for one look
at what was dearly left.

To be transformed to stone
's a hard fate, but salt
has a certain savor.

The deer must have come for miles
by moonlight to lick her feet,
bending their necks sidewise
at the smoking city.

Let others fix their eyes
ahead—this whole century.
I will turn my face backwards,
with you,
though the abandoned cities burn on the night like stars,
and the salt dwindles.

DAVID FROST PRESENTS: SATAN ON THE CRUCIFIXION

"Spectacular is the word. But then you know
it had its pedagogic side. To see
all of those kind church people holding up
my best masks to their faces, as children do
on Halloween, and grinning grotesquely down
on that poor wretch like some wierd hall of dreams
(till he must have thought he'd died, and gone
to Hell) was worth a trip. And those two thieves,
spitted against an April sky like roasting
turkeys, who with their last breaths mocked
their brother's agony, shouting 'King! King!',
were not just common men. And there were lessons
in the last words: 'Forgive them, Father,
for they know not what they do,' or better still
'O God my God, why hast Thou forsaken me?'
And the existential longings of the last word.
These things impress, but the crude jugglings
with scientific fact—the dark, the thunder,
the proceedings after—If God had hung
upon that great wine-press, and down the wood
had rolled the very heart's blood of the world,
do you think that I, who have some knowledge of
the fine points of revenge, would not have guessed,
and spent at least one night beneath the tree
in sweet memorial, remembering pain.

"Stealing the corpse out of its bed of sleep
was a cheap trick, and all the ballyhoo
and Madame Blavatsky sleight-of-hand—the ghost
who showed them where to drop their nets, and ate
wheat cakes, and doubting Thomas with his fingers
stuck in the wounds like Horner's in his plum—
surely these are children's tales. My friends,
we must comport ourselves like human beings
and give a passing nod to reality.
Be advised—myths are mythical. Now, half a nation
centered in this Eve-debauching eye,
let me strip the tree of knowledge. No fire
awaits your bodies underground, no tryst
with endless pain, just as there is no pleasure
banked in the sky, but space—the molten stars.

Resolve yourselves into your human meanings.
Christ was a famous man; and when you turn
the knob of your television, and the screen
shrinks to a tiny square of grey, it is
the last of this poor Devil you will see."

And where her shadow was, was sun—
And fear had lost what song had won.
By love consumed, by doubt deceived,
he turned—to air, and he believed.
That lyre was helpless now which wet
the Furies' cheeks with tears of jet;
and second knocks on Hades' door
made all that monster's dog-heads roar.

He turned again, and found that land
where Faith forgets her either hand;
where Time (by love) tears limb from limb
those lovers who would halter him;
and Pain alone has songs to save
the singer from the living grave.

In the horse's belly,
it is damp, viscous, slippery
as your own throat.

(The horse is not made of wood.)

We have lived here years,
but still recall the plan—
to creep at nightfall
out through the little door in the horse's side,
unbar the gates for the army
and sack the town.

But when night fell
(or what we thought was night)
there was no door—
though there must have been a door,
or how did we get here?

A question pondered daily
for years,
                though now
irrelevant.

We are old inhabitants,
used to the chewed-up food, the acrid water,
the sour half-light.

In the world out there,
the city has either fallen
or not—
our friends gone home triumphant,
or lie on the plains, old bones.

Whichever—
it happened too long ago
for us to care.

Here in this world inside
we think of the horse—

how he is grazing deep in a thick green meadow
up to his flanks in grass,
or running with a loping canter
over rock-strewn fields,
or on an ocean headland standing,
black nostrils wide, mane
blowing in the wind,
breathing the salt blue air of far-off horizons—

and we
are inside the horse.

—Hangs on the wall, a trophy, gathering dust.
Once only, when all the house lay sleeping,
did he lift it from its peg and try to bend
the darkly polished yew—until the veins
stood out on his forehead, and the blood throbbed
in every vein—and failed—And once again
threw all his strength against that stubborn wood,
till the muscles writhed on his arms like snakes,
and his eyes became stone-blind—then hung it back,
high on the wall, an emblem of the past.

No suitors swarm the house. His agéd wife,
the symbol of faithful love, remembers no one—
not even herself. The servant's dead. The dog
who died at his feet has died since many times.
A thinking man, he knows time's ordered ways,
and adjusts himself to ever-lessening powers,
not harkening towards the white horizon's sails
or the sea gulls with their mocking seaward cries,
but sometimes in dreams as in a mirror sees
the great bow bend, the suitors fall, the palace
swim with blood—and farther back, great Troy,
that vanquished city, rising in black-plumed clouds,
and feels one well-aimed arrow pierce his heart.

—And when he felt those horns
branching from his head,
                          he leaped the wind.

The dogs were quick to catch the scent. Their cries
joined with the bugles braying in his wake.

Each voice he knew by heart—
                          But when he turned
and saw those blood-shot eyes, those frothing tongues,
those mouths that grinned like caves,
                          how strange they looked!

Like pickets in a fence the trees flew by,
and brooks and glades like faces in a dream.

Too brief the hunt. New to his subtle limbs,
he stumbled on a clump of pine and fell
within a ring of teeth.
                          The dogs moved in—
to claim their master, fellow-beast and prey.
"Actaeon, where are you? Join the hunt!"
His friends came rushing up, their faces masked
with sweat. He tried to call—to tell them who he was—
and made an odd bleating. "Actaeon, join the hunt!"
The dogs moved in, snarling. For beast and man
his body bled. A spear-shaft blocked the sun;
and through a veil of blood he saw, too late,
this world has many names, masks, shifting forms,
and what we are alone is not enough.

First, that you made me weak. Oh very sound
in body—oak-limbed and awkward as a tree
that sheds its roots to walk upon the ground—
but slow in brain, shackled to analogy.
The flowers she picked you should have made me see
were different from the child, and in the lake
might float like stars, but childish gaiety
would sodden, wilt, and fail to come awake,
although I picked whole fields of flowers for her sake.

And second, that you made me ugly—all the dead
to choose from, and this the assembled face,
so stitched and marred the mirror turns its head
each time I pass, and time moves up its pace;
yet, like the gods, infatuate of grace.
I carried Beauty into the darkest wood,
but even the blinds of night could not efface
the sun's derision, no more than murder could—
and that face knelt with me to wash its hands of blood.

And finally, that you failed to understand
what you had made, but with steel bars and lies
half-verified the patchwork of your hand,
and then—at last—let fear invade your eyes;
so, broken-necked the monster-maker lies.
If I knelt down, my mouth against your mouth,
and breathed with all my might, would you arise,
and through those spells that charmed the jaws of death
make me again, a man, with some more God-like breath?

LAST WORDS OF DON QUIXOTE

"I am no longer Don Quixote de La Mancha"

All the heroes have turned
into sheep. All the ladies, the lovely ladies
to serving girls.
And all the giants
to windmills.

The enchanter has waved his wand.
The enchantment's
through.

One suit of wrinkled armor
I bequeath to the moon,
one splintered lance
to the waves,
one mud-bespattered shield
to the mockery of crows.

Trees melt on the hills.
Hills fade off into clouds.
Shadows
            turn
to shadows.

It is time to be serious, to abandon
folly, to seek out
the soul.

Tips of oaktrees blaze
in the obsequies
of sunlight.

White faces peer
through the loopholes
of stars.

And again—
the quest begins.

Without the magic of names,
stripped of all masks, dreams, disguises,
I must encounter
the real.

III

SONGS AND OTHER MEASURES

BELL SONG

Into the mouths of bells
we vanish, one by one.
The hours toll the faces
into oblivion.

Like snuffed out candles winking
into the great, blue dark
we disappear, we vanish,
leaving behind no mark.

Except for the echoes rising
out of the mouths of bells,
making the dense air tremble
with their long farewells.

Then let those great bronze clappers
beat on their metal hides,
and send the echoes pulsing
over the countryside.

Mourn! Mourn for us all, you hours
that mark the time of day,
and in your bronze-tongued mourning
wear the world away.

THE PAUSE

The crow sits on a jutting stone
above a field of snow—
one black, heroic period
in a world of flow.

Then flaps his wings and lumbers
into the air, to fly—
one small, black dot dissolving
in an endless sky.

THE FLIGHT

Swallows front the dying sun.
They perch in rows upon black wires
watching that orange disc drop down,
breasts flushed with his gold afterfires.

Weeks of soft, aching dusks they're there,
strung out like beads in silent rows,
and then, one dusk, the wires are bare,
and they've gone—wherever summer goes.

Nothing is done that is not forgotten.
Open your eyes and let them flow.
Each tear that drops is a stone fallen
from the stairs of sorrow.

The heart aching is the heart mending,
and heart-broken is a new birth.
The rising and falling have no ending
even under the earth.

White wings, unfurled, snare the sunlight—
then darkness on the wings of the dove;
so the shadow falls struck in the night
by darkness above.

There is no dam in the ethereal river.
Narcissus could not bear that glass—
the dropping image cracks the mirror
and present time endures its past.

Then bow your head—shoot your arrows,
tears, into the moving deep.
Lay down your bow and search the ocean—
no shafts, an empty quiver.   Weep!

THE ENIGMA VARIATIONS

Lying in the dark music,
thinking of faceless friends,
or those kept whole but marred
by envy or turned self-hate,
and Father's upturned face
fishing the lily ponds
of pain, alone, the moon
bandaging his head,
and all good children grown
up to the four winds,
tears move upon my face
like half notes on a sheet,
and I would be a grave
walked on by stones to keep
even a mouldering faith,
though time is the heart of music.

REBUTTAL

Once I had all the answers
to prove this strange life good—
to justify God's ways to man,
man's ways to God—
and lived in an abstract ecstasy
of brotherhood.

Grown old, now all those answers,
like wax in a candle's flame,
dribble into an endless void
of grief and pain,
and back come all the questions
from which the answers came.

BURNING THE LOVE LETTERS

Long smouldering passions, waked to flame—
See how these pages twist and turn,
tormented by love's fiery tongues,
and in their antique ardors burn.

Bodies of lovers, twisting, turning,
in a carnal holocaust of gold,
condemned for witchcraft, heresy,
for fires once crimson, now grown cold.

Condemned to Paradise,
I walk these glittering streets
scorched by the love in every face
my face must meet.

Crying for mercy mocked,
for justice scorned, undone,
while down my cheeks the tears of grief
and mercy run.

To prove my God a man
whom once I thought a king
I died, and through these streets his voice
comes echoing:

"Dark shadow of the sun,
dear, necessary shade—"
and once more, by the wiles of love,
I am betrayed.

And pride become mere folly,
reason and honor gone,
I wander here in hopeless joy
the fool of song;

And only when I remember
look back on earth and see
betrayer and betrayed still hanging
from the one dark tree.

Dear Beast, your beastliness melts down
the marrow of my bones.
Such passion, and such poverty
could melt a heart of stone.

Then in my arms transformed, a Prince,
what drove my body wild
lies beautiful, lies innocent
as a sleeping child.

But turned away in dreams, once more
that darkly pillowed head
becomes a strange, a savage thing—
alone, uncomforted.

And the room shrank to a matchbox—
the bed turned small,
the lamplight dwindled until it seemed
no light at all—

and each of those tiny faces
hovering overhead,
dropping their small, enchanted pearls
upon the bed

seemed infinitely far-off, fragile
as dollhouse things—
lost in their little griefs, their hopes
and sufferings—

Absurd, in a house of make-believe,
to shed real tears—
over such minute tragedies—
such imagined fears.

AFTER FINDING A SPIDER BUILDING A NEST IN HER HAIR

Grown old—but not so old as that!
Spider, what do you think you're at—
Building a nest within my hair
to shame the grey that time set there,
presumptuous as Arachne still,
braving the gods with your small will.

Believe it or not, once I could catch
spoils of my own in this grey net,
and by a fine-spun, magic art
snare in gold strands the human heart;
but moon by month, and time by tide,
the strands loosened, the magic died.

Now caught in a web more finely spun
by a greater spinner, I lie among
old trophies, wondering at the strength
of each thin thread—its girth and length—
and with a light hand brush you down.
Go weave in the dark your silver crown.

THE CANCER PATIENT TO HER DEAD HUSBAND

For M.B. & R.B.

For three long years I have practiced the art of dying.
In one month, you are dead.
Quick march, like the soldier you were, scouting enemy country
you have stolen ahead.

You who were my stay through those slow, blank midnights
when the suffering grew too much,
and only your pain in my pain gave me courage to bear it,
the strength of your touch.

Was it my long dying that wore you from the land of the living,
or just some foolish jest
that after all these years of mourning me, my going,
you should go first?

Sheer strength of will held the sun, hours past its setting,
on the rim of the fiery sky.
From too much love of the light I could not let him
drop down and die.

Now, tutored by your swift passing, I can see him tumble
into his cold, grey bed
unmoved, the daylight so much less lovely, more lovely the darkness
now you are dead.

As silence brings to the witness sounds
too subtle for the active ear—
dim furnace sounds, the sounds of lamps,
vibrations on the quiet air—

so loneliness, like some opened door,
admits the echoes of the past—
echoes of those once loved, long gone—
the conversations of the lost.

Sounds of your own dead selves, the sounds
of children growing beyond the walls,
night's flittery sounds, the sounds of feet
tiptoeing down dark, silent halls.

Until this present time, its sounds,
seem but intruders in the ear,
drowning with harsh, persistent noise
those vagrant tones we long to hear;

and that strict darkness, shunned so long,
appears a refuge, where each word
spoken in that loved past still sounds
in perfect stillness, clearly heard.

As I move down to darkness,
darkness inside me grows.
All that seemed clear turns clouded—
melts and flows.

Life's purpose, once italic,
becomes a hidden task.
The face I see in the mirror
wears a mask.

And that other face once glimpsed
in the glass of lakes and stars
shatters in the wind's light ripples,
faults and blurs.

Wisdom, is this your folly—
to see through darkness' sight
those truths the sun's too brilliant shining
shrouds in night?

Always the hilltops take me,
and always I go—
over the slight green rise at the end of fields,
over ridges of blue
distance—and on—where to—none know.

Having lived more than half my lifetime,
long ago I found
how hilltop leads on to hilltop, how mountain
to mountain gives ground,
past the horizon's bound.

And yet these exultant promises
still leap in my blood,
as I stand here gazing at the far blue heads of hills,
lost in the flood
of longing—for some unknown good.

O skyward leaping hungers
you are not lies!
Though your heights give way to other hilltops rising
beyond the reach of our eyes,
you are your own eternities.

I shall rest in you—both moving
and planted here,
in these green, curving flanks, these waves of earth and stone
that cresting in air
plunge down and break—upon what far-off shore?

Under the garden sleeps the sun.
The mole burns in that fiery eye.
From the dark places, the winds blow down.

Light rots the green roots underground.
Trees shrivel up—plants, flowers die.
Under the garden sleeps the sun.

Men walk upon their heads. Someone
upturned the world. What was low is high.
From the dark places, the winds blow down.

Virtue is mocked—Violence crowned.
Nightmares breed and multiply.
(Under the garden sleeps the sun.)

Sucked into the black-holed heavens, stars drown.
The dead wake in their graves and cry.
From the dark places, the winds blow down.

Arise, O buried Lamp! Great One,
take back your kingdom in the sky!
But under the garden sleeps the sun.
From the dark places, the winds blow down.

THE SOWER

(After a painting by Van Gogh)

Sower by the slanting tree,
sun vast halo round your head,
sowing the dark, enchanted seeds
which as they fall are harvested—

Blue daubs of field, small yellow house,
green-yellow sky, light streaked with pinks,
and on the low horizon poised
a moon-like sun that rising sinks—

Dark body of a slanting tree
jutting across both earth and sky
like the body of some ancient king
stripped of his robes and crucified—

And you, beneath the tree, your arm
rising and falling like the sun,
sowing the seeds of light and dark—
eternity—oblivion.

There the sail's luxurious curve
commands a blue and endless sky.
Here a stony sun beats down
to black a world that cannot die.

There dwell the rich, bronze newlyweds,
intransients at the task of joy.
The sick live here, the lame, the mad,
and those the love of Gods destroy.

This is the country of the blind
who see the world through darkening bands,
drink in the simple leaves like moths,
and cup the sunlight in their hands.

There the landscapes riot gold,
and acts of joy bind, link by link,
the heart to perfect happiness.
Time is given here to think.

The body here is burned, to light
greater worlds of lesser day.
There the flesh becomes the soul
and ripens in the soul's decay.

Apples bend those amber boughs.
Here, the trees have night to give.
Eagles dive on burning wings.
In this country I would live.

"It will all go on,"
said the bird,
"when you and I are gone,"
said the bird—
"when black-barked, red-tipped trees
bear no more leaves,
and shoots,
green-bursting, rocket-speared,
yellow at the roots,
and our daily fire, the sun,"
said the bird,
"dips his face into night and is done,
and the Pleides, Orion,
the Great and the Lesser Bear
run over the sky's edge
and disappear,
and the First Word,"
said the bird,
"echoes in the last silence
of the first darkness
unheard,
and everything and everyone
is no one,"
said the bird,
"is oblivion,"
said the bird,
"it will all go on."

When Jesus left the tomb
he felt beneath bare feet
the glowing stones, first-touched with morning's
tender heat—

And felt the sunlight mounting,
pressing against cold flesh
to thaw from dark imprisoned bones
the chill of death—

And heard the birds of morning
pour in his wakening ear
celebrations of the sun, new-risen
from darkness' bier—

And for the first time knew
the ground on which he stood—
adjunct of Paradise, lost Eden's
hidden wood—

And saw bright spirits dancing
lightly through the body's dress,
moving from joy, to pain, to joy,
blessed and unblessed—

And dropping upon his knees
he hugged that secret earth—
the world beneath this once-born world
of death and birth.

TIME SONG

Alter one link, we vanish—
turn nothing, never were—
these solid-seeming bodies
changed to air;

or follow the dark web backwards
through mazes finely spun,
and over the first ocean see
the first sun;

or stretch a hand into the future
that down through a thousand years
will shape the lives of those unborn,
affect the stars.

And yet, like some picture woven
upon an endless wall,
it hangs—perfected—finished—
never to change at all.

IV

THE WORLD OF IDEAS

MIRAGE

At the woods' edge,
looking in—
through wells of succulent shadows,
transparencies
of green light, fronds
of gold,
an absurd hunger rises
to eat
(like some enormous moth)
into that ambrosial heart
of green.

Scratched, bitten, bruised
I emerge,
learned in old sayings—how beauty
is skin deep, how it stumbles
into ungainly fields
of potatoes and cows.

But turning
to brush away mirage—
again that exotic sight,
sweeping my whole body
like pain.

Surely
though the way was wrong—
the end
       was right.

From across the stream, on the side of the opposite hill,
I see a woman in a blue, wool coat who is walking her dog.
Her hair is as white as snow, and her dog snow-white.
They are walking through the plum-brown, silvery branches of trees.

Step after step she moves,
leaning on each foot, as the old do.
She is walking her dog and thinking.

Under the nest of her hair is another world—
are many other worlds—past, present, future—
but none of this shows.

She is walking her dog and thinking, and the dog too
is thinking—Bushes are telling damp, excited tales
of an earlier sun, of a darkness before this sun—

and the trees around them are thinking—slow, wooden thoughts
that stretch over centuries, and the earth in which the trees
root down also is pondering—deep, stone thoughts—
but none of this shows.

I see a woman in a blue, wool coat
who is walking a small, white dog
through the plum-brown, silvery trees.

IDENTITY

They are always saying, the others— "Be what you are!"

There are wolves in a dark woods running
on the track of deer.
                    The crusted snow
crunches under their paws,
their flashing hooves.
                    The wind
ruffles their fur—rubs dark their tawny haunches.
Their tongues hang down
                    red-flagging the moon.

And in the sky
                an owl makes quiet rings.

When the hunt is done
shall I lie,
lashing the hard, white snow-crust with my hooves,
lick up the pools
that sink in the frosty snow in soft, red circles,
or float in the sky,
composing the whole dark picture
under my wings?

A FOOTNOTE TO EPICTETUS

"We must learn to desire that things should happen as they do."

Bending over the handles of my racing bike,
sniffing the fresh spring air of early morning,
when Whoosh!—my front tire goes—as I desire.

Five miles from home (as the crow flies, who flies
or not just as I ask him to) I begin
to walk.

        Faint rumblings—Rain clouds in the east—
and just at that moment that I think it should,
down floods the rain,
              and sops me, head to foot.

Passing in cars, people hug their inner warmth
and pleased, stare at my rain-drenched figure—
                As I desire.

One pedal scrapes the ankle of one foot,
raising a meat-red welt. White fire runs
up and down my leg. (As I tell it to.)
The traffic thickens. With every passing car
I'm swamped by a tidal wave.

            Soaked to the skin
and shivering, hours after, I arrive back home,
and sitting at my desk write down this poem
(which is good or bad precisely as I wish)
and which you are reading now and like or not
just as it pleases you—

           And in the meantime pleasing
myself and Epictetus, who first desired it.

RECURRENT DREAM

Someone has taken us down to that supreme house
where the sundials point always to noon, and left us there,
wandering through dim gardens—geometric rows
of ripely blooming trees, green hedges, fountains
which rising up hang motionless on air—
where all things keep an obdurate repose,
except for us, the visitors, who roam
up aisle and down, abandoned to our choice.

The rooms are elegant, high-ceilinged, bare
of any signs of those we seek—our hosts.
Our needs are met, met sumptuously, and more;
and yet the unease inside us grows and grows.
Where are the occupants!—hiding in the walls,
transformed to statues, dogging us like ghosts—
till tired of waiting, like actors taking roles,
we fill their places—gesture, look and voice—
but wonder—Shall we—like them—soon disappear?
Are there guests waiting in the garden for us to come?

1

Disturbed from dreams—the cry of the great horned owl
furring the dark, as if the throat of night
had opened and given sound; a child's cries
slicing the black transparencies of sleep—
you wait, dark-watching, still half pooled in dreams.
His body trembles; huge with dark his eyes
reflect a world where through the close-meshed screen,
winged on its own voice and feathered white
in the moon, a vision comes—a horned owl—
gliding immensely in, to circle the room
and draw all sleeping children into its deep-
set eyes—a world of marvels lit by the moon.

2

Upon an owl's back our house once flew
over the snow-blanched woods, and peering down
I saw the silver-glinting eyes of ponds,
the quilt backs of the hills hunched under fear,
and plunged with the taloned sky's ferocity.
Now watching our children, while the mastodons
march the playroom floor, we fail to see
the giant fern leaves spill their cups, the ground
quake beneath colossal footsteps, and fail too
to look beyond the cloistered walls of truth—
where the horned tiger thrashes in our tears—
and smile at the games of innocence and youth.

3

Sleep has an owl's eyes and conjures forms
unseen by the blinding vision of the sun,
strange forms that live under the mushroom leaves
of the brain, swarming stalks of shadows—Down
the dark stairs it comes, and groveling in the ears
of terror we see arising from its graves
the incommensurable image—until it shears
the hasps of sight—and still we cannot run,

except from the land of dreams. In fathers' arms
sons die. Unnatural desires flaunt
themselves. Masks scramble the face of clowns.
With the red moon beasts arise and hunt.

4

The youth of man was passed under the hill
of night, hearing the wings of fireflies
big as owls, the anguished wings of trees,
and watching hooded lanterns sweep the air
in paths of death over the tangled brush;
and in the ground feeling beneath his knees
earth's heart quick-beating, earth's breath rush
shuddering in and out, while in the sky
the head of God hung, bloody-cheeked and still,
plotting the luminous fractures of all wars.
The past lives on. We are the things we were;
although we probe the head of dark like stars.

5

So much to master under the cloak of man—
such phallic wounds, abortions of the light,
such foiled hopes, such caricatures of grief—
They walk the moon-washed corridors of dreams,
wagging misshapen heads—blunt hooks for hands—
mute-tongued and pleading for the doors of life.
Must darkness be affianced for its lands?
The owl glides down the scale of dreams—Tonight
descend with the falling bird and claim again
those children you abandoned to the deep;
comfort the nightmare, sobbing in your arms—
that the sun arise, out of the grave of sleep.

"I will not take off my hat to a poem that will not die."
—*Thoreau*

Thoreau, bare-headed in the garden—
Rose petals curled in the grass—
like small pink boats
about to embark—
The lingering ghost of a smell—

No grave, no funeral.
Morticians mocked.
The mealybugs marching away.

Still-born or immortal,
the rites are the same.

Taps from the trees.
The spent light sinking
behind bare-headed hills—

and in the sky, the grave
magician bowing,

while from his black silk hat
tumble down the stars.

LATE AFTERNOON WITH CHILDREN

(After a print by Sylvia Spencer Petrie)

As supple as lilac wands they bend, all three,
over the communion of a little dog.
The boy stares off, into deep reverie.
The girl, the child look down at the little dog
(oblivious in the thick, warm, summer's grass),
smiling madonna smiles.
                              Late afternoon
lingers upon their forms, too light to pass
into blue-lengthening shadows and be gone.

That the boy, the girl, the child, the little dog
have gone—long since, passed into memory—
and the gold light waned and blazed into dying day
is of no concern to these children, this little dog
who are playing here, now, and shall always be—
too happily lost ever to pass away.

Fame, high-pressure salesman, must you come,
leaning on my doorbell like a child—
when I am on my hands and knees, fresh paint
up to my chin, and circling me like fire,
or lolling in my bathtub purged of hopes
of anything but happiness—to ring
and rout me out. And, fool, I open up,
to pick out giant laces fit to trip
Apollo's foot; or those astounding ties
only the boldest angels wear in Hell.

Is it the smile—that rainbow in the mouth
that leads to gold—or those incomparable words
you care too much about to ever say?
I buy the goods, and win the dirty ring
around the tub, the drippings on the stairs.

Someday I'll lose my patience, stumbling down
the steps head over heels, and raving mad,
slam the door forever on your foot—
to watch you hobble sadly down the walk,
muttering how the poor are never loved.

THE WALL

As out of a moat of fog,
it streamed up suddenly—
a blank barrier of white.

The car swerved
and stopped,
its left fender
drenched in the red lantern's
glow.
And his hands went cold.

There were flares, instructions, arrows
pointing due north,
and tracks
leading bumpily
into the dark
along the base of the wall,
but like the lines on maps,
the hum of tires,
the leanings of the road,
they were lies.

You could travel miles,
moving like a small beetle
along the face of a cliff,
and with long feelers reaching
into that vast white cold—

and find
          no turning.

Like a lion-tamer primped in a scarlet coat
he leads the grand procession of turning wheels.
They wave their clumped balloons and cheer; the sky
is a rich tatter of pennons and windy banners.
Birds sing in the trees. The band plays.
Head thrown back he struts, his black boots shining.
Behind, the great wheels roll, their metal rims
striking sparks in the sun.
                                     With growing speed
they move, as down some invisible grade. The band
plays. Children bounce from one foot to the other.
One hand lifted, he salutes the cheering crowd.
There is the sound of distant thunder. The wheels move faster,
till he has to trot to stay in front. The crowd
roars. The band plays. Some wag shouts out
"A Race!" and drops a hanky, and head held high
he is running, proud face taut, small beads of sweat
streaming down his flushed cheeks. The sound of thunder
grows. Faster the wheels move, faster, gathering
momentum, the sun whirling in rings of metal
speed. The crowd roars, the band plays,
the thunder swells. In earnest now he's racing,
head flung back, feet pounding the hot cement,
arms outstretched like a sprinter's for the tape.
Up on its feet the crowd is roaring louder
than the great wheels, which are moving faster, faster,
nibbling at the heels of his black boots. Like a drunken
man he lurches, stumbles—almost falls.
The noise dies from the throat of the crowd. Children
seize their mothers' hands. Closer the great wheels
come, striking sparks of sunlight. "This thing should be stopped!"
someone shouts. A groan bursts from the air—He is down!
He is down! And before their astonished eyes
over, and over, and over the great wheels go,
pressing the huge momentum of their metal rings
into that scarlet bundle of rags and man
that with each wheel's turning leaps up oddly

with a curious life, then under the next falls down—
crushed flat, bobs up, falls down—and with the last wheel's turning
       lies still.

No sound at all—over the whole length of things—
except for the great wheels moving off downhill,
and a shy whisper in the wind—
              "Poor man ...
                    Poor man ..."

"March, boy!" barked the blindman, seizing
the hard, tight curls, as if the boy were afraid,
"and lead me to my home." And he went, whistling,
bouncing a ball at either footstep,
skipping along as if time were a loser,
till the weak hands were sick with worry.
Fear was no one, and love, a younger failure.
The streets unsnarled, where grown men fear to go,
and blindmen go face-backward, but the boy tripped on,
following the sound of his voice like a tune remembered.
The night fell cold; the wind rose—too high;
but when they reached it, the whole way was forgiven.
The smells were all happy, the touches, tender masters,
and even the darkest feelings knew their names.
He loosened the curls, which scrambled warm through his hands
and heard the door that closed the catch of memory,
and it was all round and friendly.

                               But over the shoulder,
how the land grows smaller and smaller and goes enchanted.

More time was lost than weariness could afford,
groping for that house, big as a chestnut.
The knocker broke in his hands, the knob was candy;
and though through the keyhole he heard the welcome laughter,
that night, while the boy lay snug in a sleepy head,
rats made a snow nest in the hair of the blindman,
and a cold wind, coveting his rags, came in.

THE GREENHOUSE

A boyhood dream come true—

I am standing in a heaven of windows,
my pockets full of stones.
December's sun slants through.
There is a strange stillness, a breathless hush
over all—
I can almost feel the skin of the clear glass
tingle.
        I cock one arm
and throw—
          A glazed square
erupts—The glass comes shivering down—pleasure
runs down my wrist like blood—
            And again
I cock my arm
and throw—
          Smash, shatter, tinkle—
Splinters of glass stream down—
And soon in a frenzy of windows
I'm hurling handfuls of stones,
and around me the glass is falling
like hail.
        Back and forth my arm moves
like the arms of the Gods.
Through the jagged rents in windows I'm hurling stones—
at the sun's face, at the far-off faces
of stars—
and they're all breaking like windows, light shattering down
like hail—
        and sun by sun the sky
is darkening—

        But my arm tires,
my hand hangs like a stone,
my whole body is covered with small, red wounds—
and wakening—

I am standing in an ocean of glass.

Through a lattice of holes,
the sky is peering down.

Around me, already, the flowers are beginning to die.

THE MARGIN

One foot from the road's edge   inches
shy
                    of that green, grassy margin,
a smashing roar
crushed the back of his spine and crumpled his whole
        hindquarters.

Seconds late I am there,
looking down from the height of the well.

The feet twitch still,
running for that grassy island
almost gained,
and down through the stiff-glazed pupils of the eyes
I float
like a distant cloud.

No feeling in mind or body—
only a numb surprise, a dull panic
and a salt taste on the tongue,
as out of his mouth he oozed like a small, red flower.

I eased the stiffening body to the edge of the road—
to the funeral of maggots and flies—

and walked through that sweet-scent morning of early May
like a drifting cloud,
like an unspilled tower of blood.

Hunts—through clear glass windows—
blue jays, chipmunks, mice.
Heaves up beneath curved palms
fur so softly sleek
the caressing hand delights.

Plays endlessly, preens
endlessly—on paws as pure
as milk eats from the kitchen
counter pellet-meat,

and hides from children's wars
under sofa caves and chairs,
ears slant and tail atwitch.

Kills nothing, fathers no one,
hones its claws
on the back of the red love-seat,

or sleeps, curled up in balls,
dreaming of hot pursuits
on running feet.

And shut, by chance, outdoors,
crouches under the leaves
of the rhododendron—trembling
at the shadows of wind and sun.

Is pampered, prospers, lives long,
has no fleas.

Heat webs the thick green trees. The light grows dim
like an oil lamp turned down. We float becalmed
in a fetid pool of heat where nothing moves,
but all is about to move.
                              A distant rumbling—
a sudden flash—The sky breaks like an egg!
And with a faint hissing the wind begins,
first in the far-off branches of the trees,
then louder, closer—leaping from branch to branch
like fire. The drapes blow in, bulging like sails.
The roof, the walls, the windows begin to speak.
Rain comes down in gusts—white sheets. Roads
are covered with surf. Pools in the clay-baked grass—
Heads of flowers bend—
                              "Look, Look!" we run
to the flowing windows—Fissures of light grow down
like the roots of trees—The TV fades—The electricity
goes. In the neon dark we sit, excited, staring—
watching the illuminations of the rain
leap off black pavements, the green lake of the grass,
the manic heads of trees, and feel beneath us
something begin to loosen, stir, and move—this house
launched out—floating—on the coming stream of things!

THE GREEN GODDESS

"Man is in love and loves what vanishes, ..."
—*Yeats*

1

Flung nets of scent—sweet lily-of-the-valley air,
enticements of cherry, tinctures of flowering crab,
warm lilac fragrance, fragrance of flowering pear,
the promised smell of the not-yet fallen rain—
all lure you out, into the light green web
of her body, as if you might live there
always—free of misery, free of pain,
wrapped in a silken wonderment of green,
an emerald ecstasy, almost too sweet to bear.

2

Though spring is a season, summer a passing spell,
Lady, I am too happy in your arms,
lapped in the embrace of flowers, the tender swell
of the newly opening buds, and listening
to the criss-cross songs of birds, the gathering swarms
of the honey-bees—immersed in the beautiful,
too lost in the sensual joys of awakenings
to remember that all wakenings end, and spring
leads on to summer's shade, as summer leads to fall.

3

The tulips shine—red lanterns through the trees.
The tulips fall—spent petals in the grass,
their proud, sharp foliage sunk in a brown disease.
Even within the luxurious heart of May
that seed ripens, which makes all ripeness pass.
The blossoming time is a time of obsequies—
all growth a swelling outward, toward decay.
Death loves the sun and burgeons in its rays.
From the arms of spring, fall blooms, and stark December's freeze.

4

A flurry of blackbirds—starlings in a wood,
warring for seeds, wings beating, beaks like spears

stabbing in and out, their gold tips tinged with blood.
A chipmunk, fleeing, dives beneath a stone.
A cat crouches, pounces, plays, devours.
Eat and be eaten—is the simple brotherhood
of nature. Arising from field and wood hear the moans
of hundreds of tiny creatures—hurt, alone,
dying. This lush-green, prodigal world is not the good.

5

Strip off the green dress—find the skeleton,
(The bare bones stir, uneasy in their leaves)—
and dance the dance of loss till the dance is done.
All living's dying. Motion's at the heart of life—
and every motion leads on—towards our graves.
Goddess, enchantress, here on your blue-striped lawn,
among your gold-touched flowers and flowering light,
lengthening with long shadows towards the night,
I can find no peace in shadows, no comfort in the sun.

6

Somewhere—beyond this world—there is a place
which is no place, a time which is no time,
where sun and shadows blend and interlace,
motion and stillness meet and make one thing.
There, in that garden, each flower wears a face,
each earth-clod, every pebble bears a name,
and birds sing because of the songs they sing,
nothing blooms beyond its own rich blossoming,
and ends and beginnings join, body and soul embrace.

7

Yet Lady, here in your soft arms let me lie,
engrossed in the subtle blandishments of spring,
in love with the new-fledged leaves, the pure blue sky
(black graveyard where suns flare out, burn and fade)
an accomplice in my own life's vanishings,
knowing that with each breath you breathe you lie,
but entranced with this flickering world of light and shade,
this green phantasy you weave and then unweave—
dying as I live, and living as I die.

CHAIN

I was chopping wood when I heard it, wild and clear
across the daring interval of snow
like the cry of a newborn child. The axe fell
from my hand. The echoes cracked within my ear like ice
before a storm. I put my snowshoes on
and started out. It took an hour to find him—
behind the coop, caught in my trap for foxes,
a loon, his foot half off, his eyes bleared
with pain. I drew the steel jaws apart.
He slid to the ground. His wings shuddered twice,
and were still. I raised him up, thinking of the warmth
within. His beak fastened like a vice. My cry
rang out in silver links across the dark,
and echoed on the lake, the hills, the wind.

1

Climbing the rutted path, the lights of town
left far beneath, curled in the mist; below,
the blind mutterings of the sea; upon the right
black mountains rising with their massive shade;
and overhead—emptied of moon or star—
like an inverted pit—the sky, I found the night;
and found again what I had always known—
that when the light goes all shadows go,
and on the walls of this internal cave
the moving pictures blend and disappear.

2

I used to watch the crack under the door
for hours, curled fetus-like in bed,
the covers rising and falling with my heart,
and glimpse out of the corners of my eyes
the black closet's mouth, with all its rows
of hanging men, the window glazed with dark,
fingers of trees tap-tapping across the floor—
until the light failed and into my head
night flooded, tricked in the weird disguise
of dreams, old shadows wearing borrowed clothes.

3

Before the first Word, there was the Dark—
self-shrouding in its ministerial folds
all landscapes of the sun, fashioned to be
the imageless imago of one face,
the world's names all hidden in one name,
under one mask all anonymity.
And still behind each sunlit thing it lurks,
waiting till the limbs tire in the rigid molds
to lift them down from crosses where they waste,
back to the arms from which all being came.

Like jewels, against the velvet of the box
in which they lie, all objects come alive
and shine with a borrowed light, taking forms
from murky backgrounds, and in translucent depths
burning the night like coal. The good know
that darkness gathered lamb-like in their arms
is their defining grace, and wise men fix
their scrutiny on worlds beyond their eyes.
It bleaches the wings of swans—and makes their steps
shine on the air, although they melt like snow.

5

Letting the music roam through the darkened rooms
and rocking there, half-hidden from the gaze
of things that know me best—unfeatured, freed
from the lean mirror's silver-chiseled stare,
I grow to like it, willing more and more
propinquity with this retiring shade
that gives the outside world to me: warm homes
glowing across dark fields; lamp-fashioned trees;
and those black spaces in between that peer
so strangely at me through half-opened doors.

THE ATROCITY

Half-clothed, the young girl's body
peers over the ditch's edge.
Three grown-up women kneel
in the dried-up gully,
hands behind their backs,
heads pitched forward limply,
hair matting the earth.

Whatever the preparations
of pleas, proud silence, cries,
the blows and jeers of the soldiers,
the initiations
of pain,
they have been taken unawares,
pitched here suddenly
out of this world.

As in the famous painting
the man with his arms cast upwards
clutching at night,
his mouth a still-born cry,
is unprepared.
(Already the downward lines of the soldiers' guns
have launched those small black fists
which will strike his body backwards
into earth,
but his face is a hopeless lantern
of surprise.)

We too are unready.
Futile the rites of grief.
Not all the endless lessons
of history, newspaper headlines,
early deaths of friends,
launched out in white flotillas
of pain,
can make us ready.

The atoms of our hands
hug their tiny rings.

The world huddles
in the round cave of our skulls.

We are unprepared.

Balloons of silence rise
from these four bodies.
Limp mouths that have lost their tongues
they will not speak.
Yet wiser than philosophers,
or saints, they know everything—
all there is to know—
pitched here suddenly beyond names,
dreams, memories,
past being or non-being,
into what they are
(whatever they are)
forever.

THE LEADER

For Martin Luther King Jr.

1

Marching abreast in Detroit one hundred wide
and four blocks long, the towers of Hudsons and Kerns
blinking in the afternoon at that moving dragon
with the many heads, the undulant shining scales—
Two hours—slow motion—while boats on the river called
and the downward flow of music melted clouds—

But at the river's edge you were taken in—
the domed house held you—and the hindward body writhed
in confused exile, severed by many doors.
And though on the flowered lawns we waited hours
in knots of shadow, your voice like a trapped bird
circling that inner dome, there was no way—
only silence escaped—and redly the sun went down
sending us homeward, trailing our separate lives.

2

Now over one giant body
we march again,
many deaths below.

Up ridges of ebony knees,
the isthmus of thighs,
the chest's stilled beating,
skirting the gap in the neck,
closed mouth, shut eyes.

He stood on the porch leaning
in the late, spring air.
In the sun's rays the assassin
hid.
A window glittered.
There was a small puff in the distance—
and his shadow fell,
draping the warm pine boards.

Now over that fallen body
we march—

many lives—
           white and black—
many lives.

This bridge was a man.

3

Fear, he said, was our sickness—
white men
lording their fears in power,
black men
lost in the angers of fear.

He knew that face by heart.
At the end of the long barrel,
in the dark window's sights
he lived.
How many times inside
the world must have burst, ending
in a blind shower of glass.
When the bullet came
it entered
as an expected guest,
and passed on through
translated,
multiplied
into the many hummings
of bees.

We fear their sting.
They would change us from ourselves.
They would open the buds of our faces
like flowers.

4

Crowding my lawns the poor
wait, pressing indigent needs—
yellow, and black, and white.

I would keep them out—from fear—
but from fear
I open the door.

They stream in, eyes agape,
and stand one moment, lost
in the deep carpets.
Then everything goes—the drapes,
the hi-fi, chairs, the sofa,
stoppers from the bottoms of doors,
panes from the windows, wax-
paper, coat-hangers, rubber-bands, can-openers—
everything goes. Caught in that insane frenzy
I watch, amazed,
and then join in—
opening bureau drawers
and passing out socks and hankies
in stacks—underwear, savings bonds, fake jewelry—
unveiling the secret places
behind loose bricks,
pennies fallen down cracks—
but at last it is all gone, there is nothing left
and they go
out through the doors, hunchbacked
with goods, and down the drive,
casting long shadows.

The house is still—
with all they have taken away—
and I listen ...
then run to the door and call
"Come back! I forgive myself all
your sufferings! Come back! Live here!
Make this house rich!"

5

With the rags that Gandhi left
he unbound his eyes.
Birds flew out of his hands.
From the root of his tongue grew flowers,
and intransigent rivers.
He forgave darkness.
He forgave the sharpness of knives.

Walls can be raised in defense
against all
but those who will not raise walls.

March past him now where he lies
in a curious manger.
Unwind the swaddling clothes. Tear them
into small scraps.
They will bandage
the wounds
of the world.

6

The good remain.

All of our lives they are here—
behind the small print
of newspapers, in the foliage of trees,
on corners loitering, under postage stamps
or staring
from the windows of trains—

They transform sunlight
into fibrous shoots of green.
They uproot stones—
flow through the veins of the air
like winds.
They empower our dreams.

For the man who died,
mourn.
For the living man
give thanks.

7

(And yet through the burial gates
walk softly—

There are gaps in the bodiless air
nothing heals.

For the widow and the small boy—
the long dispersals of love.

Leave them alone by the crypt,
pressing their faces numbly

against the cold stone.
How many nights the house
will awake to empty rooms.
How many days
the doorknobs turn in vain,
the mirror
lose faith.

Drop flowers
into the mouths
of wells
for the one who is lost.)

8

That I say what I cannot know—
how doves took the coffined body
and flew with it up through clouds,
past rings of suns,
past night,
till feeling the tug of their small
wings' ache
he got out and walked ...
and there at Heaven's edge
all of the world's marchers
flowed down,
waving the bright placards
of paradise: "We shall overcome"
"There is a balm in Gilead"
"I had a dream... I had a dream... I had a dream"
and at the head of that one
vast body, black and white, free at last
singing he passed over
into the promised land—
is true,
is true,
is true.

THE CANNIBALS

Autopsy of oranges—the soft
devouring of flesh.

Like grace-notes, trills, the birds
drop from the morning branches
and eat.
Small twigs knock on the eaves.

Beside my plate
my mother's letter lies,
full of the dead and dying,
and the small mouthfuls
of hospitals.

I feel them as I eat,
dropping into the bruising dark like fruit—
all childhood's faces.

Outside, the wind
batters the small bird-feeder against the walls,
and bends the great-branched oaks until the wind
becomes the trees, the trees
the wind.

I snap on television.
Melina Mercouri's face
shines from the screen.
"My one great love ..." she says,
and her goshawk eyes swell huge
with tears,
and through the walls of my face,
the walls of the room,
her life shines
like radium.

I am sitting by my window watching television,
while oranges spurt in my mouth, while childhood's faces
drop into the bruising dark like fruit, and the wind outside
is bending the great-branched oaks until the trees
are one with the wind, the wind with the trees,
and all things in the world are passing slowly
into each others' bodies in joy or pain.

For months this naked lady, newly bathed,
has lain upon my walls—
                              untouched.

The softly tilted neck, the nippled breasts,
the sweetly rounding thighs—
For months this lady
has lain here on my walls
                              untouched
and yet possessed.

And now again into that secret room
I glide,
        and with no hands unlock
the forms of joy—
                        not only the woman's body,
but the little girl kneeling before the chest
in a white cascade of spring,
the brown-white dog
                        curled on the rumpled bed,
and the orange sunset perched on the yellow sill.

How blind we are—
to chase one naked creature through the world
when all creation's forms
lie bare—
            rocks, hills and trees,
                                    the wrinkled
faces of the old,
                    the bodies of moon—sun—stars—
awaiting one look,
                    one sign
to give up all their richness to our arms.

POEM FOR JOY

1

Light knocks on the door
and turning
the last corridor of sleep
I stumble up,
groping for the brass knob.
In warm, flowing panes
sunlight falls
on bare feet, arms and shoulders,
flashing the whole bright morning
into my eyes.
Tucked in the screen door,
all gold and cellophane,
is a telegram,
and hands trembling
I break the seal
and read
(It is not my birthday)
"Congratulations, dear boy!
You are alive!"

2

Birds are its native ciphers—bobbing pertly
on the jewelled lawns, or perched
in the green languors of trees,
eyes threading
the minute jungles below, so alertly poised
all motion
seems arrested there, all speed—
allegro—presto—prestissimo!—

or with spread wings embracing
the blue expanses of the sky—
"What larks, Pip, what larks!",
what pranks of gravity,
what proclamations of joy—

or hovering—condensing the sun's meaning
to gold.

Take it down, small scribes,
from memory,
how wading the slant lawns
of morning
the box of scent opens
and they are there—

the incredible miles, the long-forgotten years,
the far-fetched countries;
or racing the superway
how the white houses burst
backwards into shine,
like upturned vessels of light;
or the wind's feel, velvet,
many-bodied;
the taste of salt spray;
or how there emerges
at the end of the tunnelled windings
of the ears—a god
walking on the white mountains
of sleep.

There are places you cannot reach
with your hands—peripheries
of unmeaning too meaningful
to be vexed to truth,
though trusted in more truly
(while the fit lasts) than truths.

Through the downward force of tears
they may come,
as if you had broken through
the bottom of suffering
through suffering's own weight
and slipped past
shining
to the other side;
or like first love in plays—
suddenly
with a swift unmasking

of all things:
names fly up—
hopes drift—
happiness is too light—
and up you go floating
over the last horizons
of your eyes—
                    a small blue speck
                              waving
"bon chance."

Though they go and leave you—
open-mouthed,
holding a ring of space,
like a bowl of flowers
from which the flowers are gone.

                    5

Once down the streets of summer
a small boy rode
singing.

Raining for days and days there was no reason
for singing, and so he sang
both loud and clear.

The people on the sidewalks stopped to stare,
watching the bard go by,
no hands, singing.

And the more they stared the more that singing
rose, though the road dipped down—
steeper—darker—

And faster the boy rode, faster, gliding under
vast hummocks of night
from which lean heads

groaned up as from the fastness of the dead,
staring in unbelief
to see a boy

sounding the illicit heresies of joy,
there in that place
singing.

The road narrowed, stopped, and he was riding
through oceans of unmade sleep,
fathomless, dark,

where no thing was—shape, motion, spark—
but what he made
singing.

For from his mouth small trails of bubbles rose up shining
like stars; and the sea shrank back
as he made the world.

THINGS

In the stillness of unlife—how beautiful!

Books in their colored backs—the upright walls,
so purely strong—
shoes by the bed, clothes draped across the chair—

Not even the sun with all its magic fingers
can coax them into life.
                    Buddha himself
was not more calm, more emptied of desire—

And yet, from a great distance, motion slows—
the sun stands fixed in the sky, the sea stops,
and even our petty acts turn grave and sculptural—
the past one granite frieze upon a tomb.

Do things also ... ?
                    And even as I look,
the shoes grow tense with waiting, clothes swell out
with their future rounded bodies, and all four walls
go marching across the room, upon their shoulders,
the ceiling, like the body of a friend
just dead,
                    and books cry out,
through all their darkened words, "Be wise! Be wise!"

1

Trapped on this porcelain ledge—
mortality—
the coiled leavings of time.

The warmth of your own body
rises—
   effluvium of decay
that drove the last angels from Paradise.

Summon the flood!
Pull down the glass knob
and send
these used remains
into the winding rivers
of the dead.

2

Convictions of the animal.

Cows in their baggy skins,
lurching down rutted lanes,
heads uplifted, making their body music.

And dropping as they move
enormous pies,
   ridged cakes,
on which small wingéd things alight
and feast.

3

Great Jove
  (stupendous cloud)
hid in a black bull's hide—
from love,
  in love,
   for love.

And moved over cadenced hills

in his bossy might,
trailing his undercarriage through the tall, damp grass,
toppling heads of flowers, spilling bright globes of dew
and bawling—
from love,
        in love,
                for love.

4

Conversations of centuries—
Vermeer and old Jan Steen—

That loutish woman sprawled in her drunken sleep,
bending with her body's weight
the great gold frame—

and this cool-gestured lady,
lost in the blue-gowned sentiments of light,
perusing her sweet love letters—

Emanations of the bodily—
Duplicities of truth.

5

Oranges in pebbled skins
juice-tender, ripe—
the small green worlds of grapes,
mist-clouded, bursting—
the burnished throb of plums—

So gladly the feel of things!

Treetops, leaf wands, swaying
in the pliant wind—
                The feathered plunge of birds—
                        Fleece-strolling clouds—
Now—
        Matters of a moment—
                now—
and praise.

6

And the incendiary touch
of pain—
                    Black fire in the bones—
The mind collapsing in like a spent star—
Ribs metal hoops—
                            Hammers upon the walls—
Windows shut—Doors locked—Behind the eyes
panic pacing, horse nostrils flaring, hooves
stamping the floors—the smell of smoke—the first few yellow
tongues—

            Run at the walls—head down—
                                    and burst
from this tent of skin
                    into air—

7

The ox hangs from its hook—
red manic weight.

The cavity of its lungs exhales
the dark.

Stripped of its rind of skin,
its eyes and ears, the false mask of its face,
it hangs down in its primal energies,
grave as Lear,
            so real,
it shoulders every presence from the room.

O fierce, denuded ghost!

8

Spirit of walls,
holding with tight-clasped hands
these whirling atoms
still—
Earth spirit, creeping like a mole
through the moist-packed, root-veined dark,
preparing the beds of graves and resurrections—

Sun spirit, with the space-long arms
of gold—
                    and all you lesser powers—
spirit of pencils, spirit of hanging
clothes, opening and shutting spirit
of venetian blinds—
my thoughts move through you,
                              touching your inner forms
as a child touches the face of a sleeping friend.

9

Hard-hearted ghost,
demonic element—

And you, capricious glider through the air—
essence of lakes and streams—

Condense the cloud—
Stuff all its silver vapors in one span.
Unbind the stone—Let its secret rings
uncoil—

        A stony cloud
floats in its earthen sky.

10

One spirit moves the spirits
of this world.

Crumbling is its change of form—
its way of moving through unused space
and time.

Body, we have been this thing "myself"
too long—
            this "I"
                      which is now crumbling.

(Pain is the bell
that wakes us into morning.)

Late blessings on us both,
                              who were one thing,
as we stand here now upon this station platform
waving—
              (among the bustling porters, the moving people
saying goodbye)
                    to all
                          that we once
were.

Bathing her feet
in the milk-white light
of morning,
a young girl sits on the bed.

Through the window, trees
reach out in an ambush of buds,
baptismal whistlings.

One touch, one look—
and the world is about to open,
like an emerald fan.

But sudden as a wind
comes evening.

          The sun
sinks—Woods are
a thicket of eyes—
Trees marry their shadows—

And the moon peers through the pane—
white-faced
with memory.

On a closed-in porch
divided in oblong squares
of sun and shadow
she sits, straight up, not rocking,
wrapped in her shawl,
her feet together planted on the floor,

watching the birds
pursue their noisy purpose in the trees,
silhouettes of cars,
blue, green and flashing on the far-off road.

It is after breakfast. The sun is clear
and cool. The air is still.
She sits, not rocking,
lost in no reverie
of any past or future time
not here,
too purely what she is
for loneliness, too wise
for dreams,
             and practicing
the art of casting shadows in the sun.

RAIN

And now a son is falling,
crumbled by disease;
and now a daughter, mastered
by pain;
and parents, uncles, favorite pets and trees,
all falling
in floods.

The deeper you go in the years,
the deeper the rain.

Behind blind windows you watch
dismayed,
as the puddles swell into lakes, the lakes to seas,
who once would have run in the streets half-naked
and bathed.

To need such watering,
what endless acres of seed
underground!

Imagine that vast ocean
below,
thrashing on the black rocks and moonless sands,
in whose conglomerate body
we shall one day be.

DEATH WARRANT FOR A SMALL NAME

1

One on the wall drips blood
from hands and feet,
and one in a white flower sits
past suffering,
but with one voice they sing:
"Come out of the cave of yourself—

                        find your Self,

and be free, whether you die of love
or wisdom."

2

Here in the downward season—
where the keys unwind and you hear
the soft chirrings of death,
where moths strip the clothes from the trees,
where the ends of fields shine through—

                        it is time

to summon your hopes.

They stand—knee-deep in leaves,
reciting the lines you know
from memory,
like children saying poems—
and the leaves mount to their lips;
or like ripe fruits they fall—
one here, one there—though you run
to catch this globe while that one
plunges to earth,
brusing itself into mould—
and soon in a swooning of worlds
everywhere they're falling,
and with bewildered hands you stand amazed
in a hail
of death.

When the mounds grow hills, the hills loom up, black
                        mountains,
it is time for the real.

The face in the mirror calls,
beckoning—
but pressing against the glass
and feeling down the cold
void
you discover
a bereavement of doors.

Where have you gone, little fox,
to what dark glade?

The tracks lead into the draw,
through a pine stand, and over
the steep bank of a stream
to a hole.

And around the mouth of the hole
there are feathers, fur, small bones,
and pricking the inner gloom, twin loopholes
of fire,
and from the dark mouth rising
the odor
of decay.

4

How sick of ourselves we grow!—
of envy, cowardice, greed,
self-hate,
and the mirror's endless, crying—
"Admire me!"

The world lies outside.
Winds blow through the chinks.
Through cracks and crannies
                              light falls
from its martyred suns.
But trapped in our little names
we live in the dark delusions
of fear.

As a child turns a snow-globe,
once someone turned the world—
and still all things are falling
in a blizzard of leaves.

We rake them in towering heaps
and sit—all night,
watching the tireless flames.

5

The one on the wall says: "Offer
the hunted thing to the hounds.
Let him find himself in their mouths."
The one in the lotus flower:
"Move through the dwindling corridors
of fall
so wisely you dissolve
into air."

Wherever you are, white face,
be ready to die.

In their chapels of grass the flowers
melt without names,
and crickets sing in their shrouds.

Without malice
I shall sow you in the ground—
like a fresh-picked fruit—
like a plucked leaf—

             Fall down—
through the fibrous roof
of earth.

      There are strange
arisings
       in the land of farewell—

THE RACE WITH TIME AND THE DEVIL

You fail to win.
They are trained racers.
With five-pronged fork
leapfrogging the ground
and foot whistling
the Devil's the man to beat;
and Time with his scythe and beard
helicopting the air
is hell on wheels.

Their handicaps are fables.
Just when you think
they are passed for good—
the flats before you
unbroken by dust—
behind, black hooves
thunder—Lap Two!

To sit and watch
them flying over,
ridiculous tail and beard,
the rim of the world
would seem the defeat
of failure.

But silence has its own gait—
the stones are racers—and you run
as you've never run
in your life before.

One view of Heaven
is a burst of speed so great
they are always racing
at the edge of your eyes—
their tongues white flags,
their faces stretched and grey,
their footsteps fading
into the whorls of the past—
those heroic losers.

FANTASIA ON THE DEATHS OF MALLORY AND IRVINE

(Last seen two thousand feet from the summit of Everest,
still climbing)

1

And the clouds came down
                            and hid them
and swallowed them up.

Two dots on the north ridge creeping
against the sky—
                            Long fingers of mist
descending the mountain's flank,
white crawling on white,
and reaching that thin, black ridge—

Into the camera's eye
the old man stares—
through the eye of memory—

"One thousand feet
I climbed up the north face,
hoping to find some sign, some last remains,
or meet them coming back—

"At the base camp below
we waited days,
necks craned, eyes straining, hoping against hope,
imagining apparitions winding down
the steep pass—

then raised two rocky cairns
and left."

2

There overhead—
                            the last knife summit soaring—
snow streaming from its crest.

Only their feet decided, only their bodies plodding
numbly on—
                    too late in the afternoon, clouds closing in.
Just before dusk,
they could feel the wind-lashed ridge
stop rising,
                    and mind and body buried
in cloud,
            knew
they were at the top.

Exaltation, conquest, triumph—
absurd.

They stood for some moments, floating
on the peak of the world,
feeling only that vague, numb floating—

then began
the long trip
down.

3

"Mallory," said the wind,
"we have folded the white sheets back,
the pillows are plumped."

No malice in the tones—
only the humble servant
of their wills.

They hung for a moment
                        balanced
on the edge of pain,
then as from a long way dropped—
like two small snowflakes
falling
into deep-piled drifts—

and what was men streamed out into the night.

4

The mountain
is a god.

Feet walk upon its crest
and leave no mark.

Embedded like mastadons
in its sheer side,
enshrined in perfect bodies,
still booted and mountain-clothed
they are staring out—
                        through ice-glazed eyes—
over the curve of the world.

"Mallory, Irvine, men who were seized by clouds,
who live in the pure white body
of a god, gaze over the world's top and comfort us,
who must meet our ends
in the white cubicles
of hospitals, behind drawn drapes, kept alive
by machines, floating in thick drugged clouds,
and looked at
through the white, distorted masks of those once loved—mirrors
of our own misery
and pain."

5

Down the mountain pass—
                        two tiny figures
gliding—
        bending in shining arcs,
                                in glittering curves,
snow flashing from their skis.

Like birds with folded wings, straight down they drop,
riding the mountain's dips
and bends,
        till the scurf of ski on snow
swells loud in our ears.

"Apparitions, phantoms, black angels of wind
and sun, tell us your fate."

Blurred shadows they hurtle by, skis whistling.
"Look! Look! they shout,"
                              waving back mittened hands,
as beyond the farthest bend they dip
and vanish.

          "But can we believe
our eyes?"

              From far beneath,
the echoes
              rising
back—

          "Trust only
the dead."

                    6

Far above—
              the mountain top.

Foot after foot we lift,
climbing.
          Already our hearts labor.
Already our lungs leap, fish-like, at the air.

The slope beneath the slope, far under the final
slope—

          We are not mountaineers.
On a frozen rock we sit,
staring at freezing hands—
                              (Will we never learn
that pleasure, comfort, pain
are nothing, that triumph's
expendable,
our ends not the ends, and only glimpses
all?)
          when under our feet there begins
a strange trembling—

inside our ears
a far-off thunder grows—
                    the rock face splits,
the side of the mountain opens like a giant door
and before our eyes—in their honeycombs of light—
stand the dead,
enshrined in perfect bodies,
looking out through frozen eyes
and speaking in one vast whisper—
"Be human—
            Follow your hopes—
                        Believe in your farthest longings.

"And if you fall full-length in the drifting snow,
great dogs will come to your side and lick your hands—
If you plunge into air, the wind
will stretch out its arms and catch you in its bulging net—
and if on some ledge far from the top you freeze
into statues of ice,
the side of the mountain will open like a giant door,
and take you in—

                    where with the wise you will stand,
gazing across the white curve of the world."

ABOUT THE AUTHOR

Paul Petrie was born in 1928 in Detroit, Michigan in an area which, at that time, was on the outskirts of the city, an area both urban and rural.

Educated at Wayne State University and The University of Iowa, he was a member of the Miles Poetry Group at Wayne, and the Iowa Writers Workshop under Lowell, Berryman and Engle. While in Iowa City he met and married the artist Sylvia Spencer, and they have three children. After a year off in Mallorca, Spain, he taught for one year in Nebraska and for thiry-one years at the University of Rhode Island, during which period he spent two sabbatical leaves in Devon, England, as well as several months in Settignano and Amsterdam.

His main vocation throughout his life has been poetry, and his work has been published in eight collections and over one hundred literary journals.

Retired now he continues to write, while working toward his final degree at that famous institution, The Academy of Goodbye.